MAN'S WORLD *digest*

No.1, being a digest of MAN'S WORLD Issue 8 / Fall 2022

Cover images: Mike Vinson
(@mdvnsn on Twitter)

MAN'S WORLD

digest #1

CONTENTS

MAN'S WORLD

RAW EGG NATIONALIST

editor-in-chief

RAW EGG NATIONALIST

editorial director

RAW EGG NATIONALIST

deputy editor

RAW EGG NATIONALIST

art director

RAW EGG NATIONALIST

deputy editor's assistant

RAW EGG NATIONALIST   *editor at large*

EDITORIAL

COPY: RAW EGG NATIONALIST

RESEARCH: RAW EGG NATIONALIST

STAFF: RAW EGG NATIONALIST

ART

RAW EGG NATIONALIST

senior art director

RAW EGG NATIONALIST

art coordinator

PUBLIC RELATIONS

RAW EGG NATIONALIST

vice president / director

ADVERTISING

GLOBAL: RAW EGG NATIONALIST

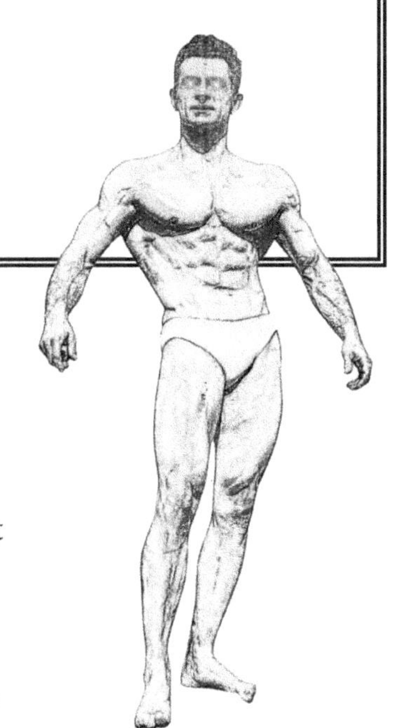

RAW EGG NATIONALIST *Your editor*

"Digest this!"

Hello, my dearest, most loyal friends. Welcome to the very first MAN'S WORLD Digest! This little package you hold in your hand — no! put *that* package away, otherwise how will you turn to pages? Anyway, where was I? Yes! This little thing is my first attempt to satisfy the persistent desire, felt as ardently by myself as any, that this fine magazine should be given a regular physical form. The logistical challenges involved in just a single man producing and distributing a magazine remain as formidable as they were when I first began this enterprise, some two years ago. So hopefully this Digest, born of compromise, will prove somewhat satisfactory, in advance of a future day when, deo volente, MAN'S WORLD will rule the newsagents' shelves from on high.

The aim here is simply to provide a fine selection from each new issue of MAN'S WORLD, in a format and style that is distinctive, but also captures some of what has become a very recognisable aesthetic in the electronic edition of the magazine.

So what's in store for you in this inaugural issue of the MAN'S WORLD Digest? Well, we start with a fantastic essay from AENEAS TACTICUS MINOR on the futility of countercultures. Then we have STONE AGE HERBALIST and his thrilling and chilling account of the life of Richard Hoskins, an academic whose life and work collided in the most fascinating, and tragic, of manners. Next we have my very own essay, "Tilting at Blackpills", which has certainly ruffled a few feathers... MARTIN provides a new translation of Ernst Jünger's early essay "Tradition", which considers a very important question for us... uh, whatever-we-ares: How must tradition guide us as we look to build a new future? HOSTUS provides us with some very perceptive remarks about the culture war and its importance. NOOR BIN LADIN interviews me about my new book, *The Eggs Benedict Option*, which is currently burning up the book charts. In the first of two fiction pieces, DETECTIVE WOLFMAN takes us back to 1950s Hollywood with a classic gumshoe story with some heavy horror mixed in. GRECIAN tells us what real grit means for Olympic weightlifters. P.C.M. CHRIST, in our second piece of fiction, imagines a human life reduced to executable code. And then last, but absolutely by no means least, JOSIAH LIPPINCOTT, bane of the woke military, tells us why we need to change our plans to infiltrate the hostile institutions that oppose us.

Here, then, is a hearty serving from the great banquet that was MAN'S WORLD Issue Eight. Digest this!

RAW EGG NATIONALIST (@babygravy9)

ON COUNTERCULTURE

essay BY AENEAS TACTICUS MINOR

What's the bloody point? asks ATM.
Countercultures basically achieve nothing.
Time for a better ideal.

You don't want to be a counterculture. You want to be a culture. The whole point of a counterculture is to replace a culture. Otherwise it's pointless. If you're celebrating counterculture for its own sake you're celebrating how weak you are. Either you've been defeated or you've failed. Or else you're lying to yourself and claiming that somehow your ghetto or your shtetl or your wasteland Indian reservation with a trailer park beside the casino and empty broken refrigerators lying around in the grass for decoration is somehow just as good as the real culture.

You want to get the fuck out of a counterculture, unless you're using it to infiltrate, subvert and dominate the dominant culture. Otherwise you might as well be like those kids you see on documentaries sometimes. You know the ones. They all have Foetal Alcohol Syndrome and sit around in Indian reservations on Friday nights with a plastic goldfish bag full of liquid diesel fuel so they can take turns inhaling the fumes through a cardboard tube.

Yep, sometimes huffing Lysol just isn't satisfying when it comes to killing brain cells and transporting you to sweet oblivion so you feel like have to get high off something you siphoned out of a pick-up truck with a straw in the casino parking lot, and then inhale it through a leftover toilet roll to prove just how little you give a shit anymore about your life or anything else. That's basically what it feels like to be proud of a counterculture. You might as well just say it openly: you're too chicken for suicide.

A lot of people used to think 'punk' is 'cool'. They still see something dangerous, manly and rebellious in punk rock because it sounds so aggressive. Old people don't understand it and tell you to turn it down if you play it too loud. That doesn't prove anything. Punk isn't cool. It's even less cool than jazz.

'Cool' as a description shouldn't be used anymore anyway. It's a debased currency, like every single other currency in this wreck of a world that was left behind after World War Two. At least we still know what it means.

'Cool' is an attitude. It shows strength, power and poise. Also manliness. It's not just a manly attitude, it's a high-testosterone, low-anxiety, low-neurosis manliness. Nothing can overpower you if you're 'cool', and when you are you have so much power over women you don't need to talk about it. They just come to you whether they like it or not. And if you reject them they're fine. They understand, even if they're bitter and resentful, and cry themselves to sleep. You were right to reject them and they know it.

If you're cool, you're fine with danger. You can take care of yourself.

Cigarettes are cool, smoking is cool, but addiction to smoking is not. Quitting smoking and gaining twenty pounds in three weeks is not cool. Getting pissed off because you haven't had a cigarette all day isn't cool either. Getting pissed off is never cool, as you know. Neither is heart disease, emphysema, lung cancer, throat cancer or being out of breath when you walk up two flights of stairs. Chain smoking is never cool, except chain smoking does sort of look cool in a movie.

Cocaine is also cool. You have to be cool to know where to find cocaine without begging people to give you some of theirs. Knowing multiple cocaine dealers is always cool, and buying cocaine properly is cool too. Especially when you pay cash for it and the dealer pretends to be your friend, and you have other people relying on you to get them high, and you spread out the powder yourself on a clean pocket mirror, cut it up with a credit card, chop it into snortable lines and then pull out a smooth, crisp banknote in a large denomination, roll it up like an expert, and offer it like a gentleman to the ladies first so they each snort a line, because secretly they're all nervous and aren't brave enough to have any without being invited.

Knowing how to find cocaine and use it is cool. Actually using it isn't cool. It makes you angry, violent and boring, and you get cold sweats and grind your teeth, and you don't know when to shut up, and either your dick gets so small you're afraid it's going to shrivel up and fall off like a wart, or else it might creep back inside your balls and go into reverse, like the dick equivalent of your belly button going from an 'innie' to an 'outie', except it's going from 'outie' to 'innie'.

If that doesn't happen, your dick not only gets hard, it gets too hard, and it's grown so much you're afraid it's going to break open the dickskin, which is stretched so tight it's starting to hurt, and there's a little blue vein running underneath and on the left side and it's throbbing painfully and you're afraid it's turned black. The whole dickskin is bright-red and shiny and you could swear it actually glows. When cocaine does this to you you probably shouldn't have sex because you already don't even want to go piss in case you end up pissing blood. Ejaculating would just make everything complicated, and so would a condom if you had to use one. The dickskin feels like a too-tight condom before you've even put one on. So you have an erection that refuses to go away and in some ways it's worse than no erection at all.

Impotence isn't cool, pissing blood isn't cool, not being able to have sex isn't cool, and neither is having a heart flutter, or cocaine chest pains, or a stroke, or severe motor and neurological damage, or not feeling the left side of your body, or fucking up your face so that it looks like you're about to yawn, but you never actually yawn, so people think either you're a retard or you had a stroke. Not everything is cool about cocaine.

Jazz used to be cool. It stopped being cool after 1920. That was when alcohol became illegal in the States. Then jazz became background music for middle-aged white people who thought they were edgy because they were going to 'secret' bars that everybody else knew about and could easily find and drank in every night. By the time alcohol was legal again in the 1930s jazz was so lame that everyone's parents played jazz records at home. Your teachers at school were trying to show off how much they knew about jazz when you were eight years old. By World War Two it was already the way marijuana is today. It was a hobby for retired schoolteachers from Denmark.

Punk never had a chance to be cool. Originally a punk was a prostitute. Then it meant boy-whore. Then it meant not just a boy-whore, but a boy who got used as a sex toy by a hobo. Think about how degrading that is. It's bad enough to be kept as a pet dick-pincushion by anybody. But if you get used by somebody powerful, like a famous Hollywood movie director or a United States Senator, at least you can almost sort of feel proud. Sure you're getting man-raped till you bleed a couple of times a day, but it's by a man who people look up to. You probably do yourself, even as their teenaged rape victim. Every night when you bite hard on that pillow you can think: one day I'm gonna rape pretty teenagers just like him. Some of his glory rubs off on you, or gets injected up your ass anyway. You hope it does, especially if you have to go to sleep with the taste of his dick in your mouth.

What's worse, getting assraped every night when you're a teenager or spending your twenties working ninety-hour weeks at an investment bank? You end up with the same benefits in the end. Also, investment banking and boy-whore pillow-biting involve pretty much the exact same people anyway so either way you end up with the same social and professional connections. In either case the rest of your life will be spent getting revenge on the world because not even homosexuals like getting fucked in the ass.

When you're a hobo's punk it's a different story. A hobo is not just poor and homeless. He's part of a counterculture too, of other pathetic single men who like to illegally hitch a ride on a freight train and sleep in a boxcar full of pig shit until they get thrown off the train, or put in jail, or just decide to leave because they see a farm where they think they can take jobs from illegal immigrants who snuck across the Rio Grande in search of the American Dream and are now stuck picking fruit for fifteen hours a day until they are rescued from their suffering by a miserable death, far away from home and everything and everyone they love. Hoboes wear gloves that have no fingers, and eat baked beans straight out of the can with a cheap stolen spoon.

We're all young once, and getting drugged and raped can happen to the best of us. Sometimes it's just unavoidable. But if you let it happen more than once, or let yourself become a kept boy, or worst of all let yourself be used as a bumsex plug by a homeless man who keeps his possessions in a polka-dot handkerchief tied to the end of a stick that he uses to beat you if you don't suck his dick, then I'm sorry to say it but you are nowhere close to cool, and I can't say I envy you for spending your moonlit nights in the middle of a haystack getting assraped.

No, there is nothing cool about punk and there never was. Not even in the 1970s when people invented 'punk rock' because they didn't have the talent to play normal music. Mediocrity and failure was built into the punk culture from the beginning. It gave molested kids a way to work off steam. There were a lot of molested kids in the 1970s thanks to birth control pills, condoms and Women's Liberation, which led to slut moms who got divorced and ended up married to stepdads who were mainly interested in teenaged stepdaughters but sometimes used their stepsons as punks when they were bored of playing air guitar in the basement rec room. It was the 1970s. People liked to experiment.

Once you understand this, all the screaming, swearing, anger, breaking shit and total lack of harmony makes sense. So does all the body piercing, tattooing, headshaving, leather with studs and general self-mutilation. Punk isn't about music, it's about yelling at the world because your mom was a slut and married some guy who put his hand in your pants. People who didn't have that sort of thing happen generally didn't become punks. Why would happy people do this shit? ◼

THE CURSE OF KNOWLEDGE

profile **BY STONE AGE HERBALIST**

From witchraft and murder in the Congo, to child sacrifice and elite paedophilia in Britain, criminologist and religious scholar Richard Hoskins stared into the abyss — and the abyss well and truly stared back into him. STONE AGE HERBALIST tells the story of a man whose life was touched by evil.

It's hard to imagine what a modern curse would look like today, how that would affect your life, but the life of criminologist and religious schol-ar Richard Hoskins comes as close as we might possibly get. His story is an almost unbelievable tale of sorrow, witch-craft, murder and adventure, the kind of life which one associates with a bygone era. Hoskins' biography touches on some of the most bizarre events in recent British histo-ry, from investigating Yoruba human sacri-fice in London to VIP Satanic sex-rings. He has lost three of his children in tragic and disturbing circumstances and undergone hormone therapy and the removal of his testicles through NHS gender affirmative care, an act he regrets. A haunted figure, a man half in touch with the supernatural and demonic. Let us explore this, a life most cursed.

Twins In The Congo

Hoskins was born in Beaconsfield, Buck-inghamshire in 1964. His schooling led him to Sandhurst Military Academy where he gained a Special Short Service Commission in the 3rd Battalion of the Royal Anglian Regiment. Not much is known about his early life, but his story really begins when he married a medic, a woman called Sue, and went with her to the Congo in 1986.

She was working for the church, provid-ing basic medical care and vaccinations to the most rural communities, and Hoskins was excited to be travelling and working alongside her, a great new adventure for a newlywed couple. Kinshasa was not what he expected. Warned that Sue would be kidnapped at the local market and sold into slavery in Dubai, and rattled by the flagrant aggression and corruption of the local regime thugs, he was pleasantly surprised when he landed in Bolobo, a small town on the Congo River in the western-most region of the country. The local Bantu tribe, the Bateki, welcomed them both with open arms, teaching them to speak Lingala, how to pilot a dugout canoe and hunt with handmade muskets. Hoskins fully im-mersed himself in the culture and his work, installing a solar powered vaccine fridge and carving trails through the bush for their battered Land Rover. He learnt about the Congolese belief in kindoki, a form of low-level witchcraft which afflicted people from time to time and the nganga healers, who would restore ailments both physical and spiritual with herbal remedies and animal sacrifices.

In 1987 Sue fell pregnant and both were troubled by the late scan which revealed twins, one positioned for a dangerous breech birth. Twins in the Congo, as in other parts of Africa, are both revered and feared, believed to be more in touch with the spiritual world. The eldest twin is always known as Mbo and the youngest as Mpia. Distressingly one twin was born dead, amid a frightening and primal labour, far away from the benefits of a hospital. The second twin, premature and sickly, miraculously survived the night. They named her Abigail.

They briefly returned to Britain in 1988, where Abigail was declared fit and healthy, but on returning to their work in Bolobo Hoskins learnt that the villagers were worried about their daughter. He was approached alone by a man called Tata Mpia, himself a surviving twin and given a warning:

'But . . .what's this to do with my Abigail? You said she was being called? What . . . what do you mean by that?' 'Ah.' Tata Mpia nodded his head slowly. 'She is a twin. She is a Mpia – a younger twin – like me.' I felt the heat of Abigail's fever on my own forehead. 'Twins have a special power, Mr Richard. They call to each other and you must listen to their call. Mbo is calling your Mpia to come and join her in the shadowlands. I am sure of it.' 'Her twin sister? Calling her? But she's—' I stopped myself. 'No, Mr Richard,' Tata Mpia said gently. 'Mbo is not dead. That is the thing I am trying to say to you. She is one of the living dead. And she is calling out to her twin sister, calling her to the world of the living dead.'

His worst fears were to come true.

Both Hoskins and his wife began to feel that something was wrong. They heard distressed voices calling out sometimes, Abigail seemed full of life but also haunted by something. As Hoskins recalls, in one of his most chilling anecdotes in an already unpleasant book:

'Abigail?' I stepped towards her. 'What are you up to?' She turned her head, and the expression on her small face – normally as bright as a new flower – made me stop dead and lifted the hairs on the back of my neck. There was something in her eyes I had never seen before. Something that made her look old beyond her years. Without a sound, she turned away from me to stare out of the window again. I realized then what held her attention so completely. This was the only point in the house from which it was possible to see the graveyard.

Tata Mpia urged Hoskins to find a nganga and have him perform a sacrifice, to placate the soul of his dead child, but Hoskins refused. He recounts watching a similar ritual and felt that he could not go down that path, no matter how tempting. Abigail died in her sleep shortly afterwards, peacefully and with no explanation. Hoskins was overcome with grief. Burying his second child next to the first with shaking hands he felt a hand on his shoulder, the village elder - 'Mr Richard,' he said, 'now you are truly an African.'

The pair came back to the UK shortly afterwards, battling with their demons. Hoskins was privately tortured by the thought that he could have spared Abigail by ordering a sacrifice; he never told Sue about Tata Mpia's suggestion. They attempted to salvage their lives and had another child, a boy called David in January of 1990. Despite this nascent familial bliss, they were drawn back to the Congo, where they continued working until the country became too dangerous for them to stay. In the autumn of 1991 an explosion of violence rocked the country, as rebel soldiers demanded their wages and went on a looting spree through Kinshasa. Sue and David fled to South Africa and were evacuated to Britain. Hoskins attempted to keep their medical centre running, but was forced to flee across the Congo River in a canoe, under a hail of bullets.

Finding themselves back home again and with Sue expecting another child, they seemed to live in two worlds. Becoming ever more drawn into his faith, Hoskins successfully applied to Oxford to read theology, but spent a month in 1992 helping the UN coordinate supply lines from Kinshasa to Bolobo. The UN offered him a job, working on the Congo-Rwanda border, as the country rapidly spiralled into warfare and mass murder. Wisely, he refused, and came back home to continue his studies.

Their next daughter Elspeth was over a year old and Hoskins was happy and relieved to dedicate himself to his studies. He achieved a doctorate from King's College London, but at this point he and Sue were practically strangers to one another. The intense grief, the travels and turmoil of their lives, combined with differing views on their religious convictions, had resulted in them both retreating into their inner lives. They divorced and separated when Hoskins was offered a lectureship in African religions at Bath Spa University in 1999. Despite having experienced enough grief and hardship to last a lifetime, Hoskins had no idea what the future had in store for him.

The Boy In The River

It was an IT consultant on his way home from work who noticed it first. A strange dummy-like figure covered in a red-orange cloth. After realising what it was and phoning for the police he stood watching as a team fished the torso of a young boy out of the Thames. He was missing his head, arms and legs and had been clothed only in a pair of girl's shorts, bright orange in colour. The police were baffled. The pathologist identified him as a 7-8 year old African male. His limbs and head had been expertly removed and his neck bore a strange surgical wound from back to front where he had been held upside-down and drained of his blood. Hoskins was a senior lecturer at this point, one of the few experts in Britain on African religious practices. He had started a new relationship with a student called Faith and the pair had moved in together after a research trip to his old stomping ground in the Congo. Scotland Yard was convinced the boy's death was connected in some way to an African religious practice, they tossed out words like voodoo, juju and muti, a South African practice which, in its darkest forms, involved using the internal organs of a person for their medical and spiritual power. In the absence of any identification the police had named the boy Adam.

To do full justice to Hoskin's involvement in the Adam case would be to rewrite his book, *The Boy in the River*, which details his specialist expertise and research into West African sacrificial practices. Adam was eventually identified as a Nigerian,

> **...he stood watching as a team fished the torso of a young boy out of the Thames. He was missing his head, arms and legs and had been clothed only in a pair of girl's shorts, bright orange in colour**

based on the new technique of assessing bone and teeth isotopes, a first in British criminal history. His stomach revealed that he had been fed a vile potion, made up of charcoal, plants and animal bones. Significantly the forensic team discovered the potion contained the Calabar bean, a toxic legume which was traditionally used as a witchcraft ordeal in Nigeria and surrounding countries. If one vomited after ingestion they were guilty, if they died they were innocent. In very small amounts the bean acted to paralyse and numb the victim. A gruesome picture was eventually painted of the boy's fate. With his orange shorts and final deposition into the river, Hoskins could infer that the ritual was linked to the Yoruba people. The shorts themselves were only sold in Germany and Austria, providing a clue as to his movements before his death. It would seem that Adam had been somehow smuggled into the country, starved and then force-fed the paralysing concoction, before having his throat slit and his blood drained. His limbs and head were removed and kept and his torso dressed and put into the Thames. Who committed this atrocity and why are unknown to this day. Despite the police travelling to South Africa and personally requesting Nelson Mandela's help in broadcasting the crime, no developments or leads emerged.

For Hoskins this case caused painful old memories to resurface, connecting the death of a child, Africa and sacrifice. His mental fragility became evident as he was bombarded with threats from angry Yorubans, furious he had mentioned their religion on the news in connection with the murder. He even had a teacher from Yorkshire phone him, shrieking that he was undermining 'racial harmony'. His life with Faith became strained as he worked long hours, absorbed in memories and pain. One day she eventually confided that a souvenir African death mask they had bought on holiday together was causing her immense distress:

Just then Faith pushed the door ajar and peeped in. She looked uneasy. 'You're going to think I'm nuts. It's that damned mask. There's something weird about it.' I'd never liked the Chokwe death mask. I'd been uncomfortable when Faith had seen it on a trader's table in the Brazzaville market. It would have been shaped around a dead girl's face so that whoever wore it thereafter might draw up the spirit of the deceased. It was strangely beautiful, but the first night we'd had it in the room with us we'd both had chilling nightmares. We'd hung it on the wall of our home in Bath, and occasionally, when I'd been working late, the thing had given me the creeps. 'I put it up on my study wall when I unpacked,' she said. 'And I've been getting blinding headaches ever since.' She hadn't told me before because she couldn't see how her headaches could possibly have anything to do with the mask. But as soon as she took it out of the room, the headaches stopped. As an experiment, she'd passed the thing on to her mother, for whom it had no connotations. But her mother had started to have awful nightmares in which the mask featured, and now she wouldn't have it in the house. 'And she smells,' Faith went on, 'of wood smoke. She always did a bit. But sometimes it's really

By 2003 Hoskins was a man much in demand. Police forces across the UK began to call him for advice regarding any crime with a religious or occultic bent

strong. Almost choking.' I didn't like the way Faith had called the mask 'she', as if it had a personality of its own. That wasn't something I wanted to consider.

Progress was slow on the Adam case. Eventually a Yoruba woman called Joyce Osagiede was arrested in Glasgow. She was wanted in Germany for immigration crimes and her evidence led to a joint Italian, Irish and British police operation which busted an international child trafficking ring based out of Benin City in Nigeria, where Adam was from.

Child Witches in London

By 2003 Hoskins was a man much in demand. Police forces across the UK began to call him for advice regarding any crime with a religious or occultic bent. He worked on the savage murder of Jodi Jones in Scotland, before being handed the case file for a Congolese child witchcraft case in London - Child B. The story of Child B is a disturbing glimpse into modern multicultural Britain: an Angolan war orphan, smuggled into the UK by her aunt and brutally tortured by her and her friends who believed she was possessed by kindoki. This wasn't Hoskin's tame jungle kindoki, this was a new and mutated form which had arisen in the darkness of the Congolese Civil Wars. Rather than kindoki being a diffuse but mostly mild form of bad spiritual energy, the new revamped version had blended with a sadistic form of Christianity, where children in particular were held to be possessed agents of the Devil.

For 8-year-old Child B this meant her guardians had beaten her, tortured her with knives and rubbed chili pepper extract into her eyes, as well as refusing her all food and drink for days. For Hoskins this was to become his new reality, and he became obsessed with finding out exactly what was happening in London. His blood ran cold when a limp-wristed council lawyer phoned him and sheepishly asked if he would sanction a child being sent back to the Congo to undergo an exorcism. Incensed, he demanded the council pay for him to go to the exact church the child was destined for in Kinshasa. To his amazement, they agreed.

In February of 2004 he flew out on a erstwhile fact-finding mission, discovering to his horror that the Congo he knew had been twisted into something unrecognisable. Tens of thousands of street children, some lying dead in the road, crowded the city. Churches were holding many of them in metal pens and sheds. They were starved, mistreated and forced to undergo violent and frightening 'deliverance' rituals, to cast out the demons. Hoskins returned again in 2005, this time with a camera crew, attempting to locate a small boy called Londres, who had disappeared from Britain. Despite nearly being torn apart by a mob during a street funeral, the team found the boy, but they could do little to help. With casework mounting in the UK, Hoskins was called to be an expert witness in the Child B case. His testimony that kindoki was a sincere belief, but one which had been warped over the past few decades, was instrumental in putting the accused behind bars.

In his fixation on child witches, his relationship with Faith began to crumble. Sensing it was near the end, he threw caution to the wind and abandoned his work, utterly despondent at the state of UK law enforcement and the reality of child suffering in the Congo. He sold their London flat and moved with Faith to Devon, near her parent's farm, where they had a son in 2007 - Silas. Four happy years ensued, a scene of rural bliss, until a police officer managed to track him down in 2011. Another child had been murdered in London. They suspected it was a kindoki case. Unbeknownst to Hoskins, he was about to walk into possibly the worst case of child abuse in British criminal history: the torture and murder of 15 year old Kristy Bamu. The Bamu children, Congolese in origin, had been invited by their eldest sister to come to London for Christmas. They arrived into a nightmare. Their sister's boyfriend, Eric Bikubi, immediately accused the children of being witches. A three day horror scene unfolded as Bikubi beat and starved the children until they confessed, but Kristy Bamu refused. After Kristy wet the bed from sheer terror and panic, Bikubi turned his attention to the teenage boy. Forcing Kristy's siblings to help, he rained down on Kristy a frenzy of violence - knocking his teeth out with a hammer, shoving a metal bar down his throat, smashing ceramic tiles across his head, mutilating his ears with pliers. At the trial the court handlers had to use two trolleys to cart in the number of makeshift weapons used on the boy. Finally, Bikubi ordered the children into the bath where he granted Kristy's last plea - "let me die". He made his brothers and sisters sit on his chest until he drowned, whereupon he sprinkled them all with the water in an act of purification. At the trial the barrister noted the sibling's disgust at their eldest sister's refusal to intervene:

'And then, when Kristy staggered across the room, blood pouring'– Altman paused, *betraying his own distress for the first time – 'all you could say to your own fifteen-year-old brother, who was dying in front of you, was, "Don't sit on the sofa, or you might spoil it . . ."'*

Yet again Hoskins had been dragged into another case of Congolese witch-craft and the death of a child, he had been chained to the country and seemed fated to be gripped by its pain.

In August of 2011 he returned, yet again, to Kinshasa, this time with another TV company to document the deteriorating situation of its children. After battling with a cold-hearted pastor to give a small toddler a glass of water, in defiance of the fast ordered by the church, he vowed never to return. He would again take the stand as an expert on Congolese religion in the Bamu trial, outraged that Bikubi was attempting to plead insanity as a defence. At this point in his story his autobiography ends, with a despairing reflection on the state of affairs:

I didn't believe that Europe was just seeing a momentary overspill of misguided religious fundamentalism. Something much worse was beginning to flourish beneath the farcical ignorance and superficiality of the pan-European multicultural agenda. Children were being trafficked and used for benefit fraud, sold into sex slavery and subjected to physical and mental abuse. Porous national borders, splintered churches, broken family ties and a fundamental lack of understanding and communication amongst the relevant authorities had fostered a litany of depravity. Victoria Climbié, Child B and now Kristy Bamu were unlikely to be the only victims.

Sex and Gender

So far we've been following Hoskins' life through his own published words, in his book. But his life after Kristy Bamu was anything but easy. What he didn't mention in his book was the fate of his children from his first marriage. It appears that his son, David, was not a well man, and at age 19 had climbed an electricity pylon and touched the 33,000 volt cable. After 42 days in hospital Sue made the decision, alone it seems, to switch off his life support. Some time after 2011 he and Faith also parted ways, leaving him fully alone with his thoughts. Hoskins, clearly a traumatised and broken individual, fell down the You-tube transgender rabbit-hole and became convinced that taking oestrogen might help him feel better. He purchased some from a dark web vendor based in Vanuatu. The side effects drove him to seek medical help and he was 'fast-tracked', in his own words, through the NHS gender clinic in 2015 and began to call himself Rachel. In 2016 he travelled to Bangkok and then to Malaysia, combining his own personal torments with his desire to track down and uncover child trafficking networks.

He returned to Bangkok that December, and paid £15,000 to a private surgeon to remove both his testicles. This clearly did not have the intended effect he hoped for, and despite being scheduled for a vaginoplasty in March 2017, he instead checked into the Nightingale clinic in London. There, he was finally diagnosed with severe post-traumatic distress, stemming from the death of his twins, his son and the police work he had been undertaking for nearly 20 years. Through intensive trauma counselling he began the process of detransitioning, taking male hormones and returning to his name - Richard. Writing in the Mail on Sunday:

For a decade, I ran and ran. I tried to escape my life, my very identity. I changed my gender to leave Richard and his life behind. Inspired by youthful images of smiling women, I grabbed the chance for a different life. I know I'm unusual and that few others have experienced the multiple traumas to have befallen me"

While not bitter, he wrote that he was incorrectly diagnosed by the NHS gender services and was never questioned as to why he wanted to change his sex. This is both revealing of how the transgender medical industry operates and of how complex trauma can lead to body dysmorphia. Tragically he will have to live the rest of his life on hormone therapy, an avoidable mistake.

As if this tale was not baffling enough, while he was in the process of transitioning towards his short time as 'Rachel', Hoskins was asked to consult on the confusing case of Operation Conifer by the Wiltshire Police in 2015. Operation Conifer was a national investigation into accusations made against former Prime Minister Edward Heath that he abused young children. This included a string of different allegations, and the final report documents inquiries into sex workers, use of maritime vessels, bodyguards and intelligence officers amongst others. Hoskins was asked to work on a particularly lurid investigation based on the testimony of 'Lucy X', who gave a description of a satanic ritual during which Heath and other figures of authority abused a young boy on an altar, killed him and feasted on his body. The police were concerned that her testimony was rational, structured and 'evidence-based', and that it should be taken seriously. Hoskins ultimately dismissed the report, citing the controversial use of hypnosis and 'memory-retrieval' techniques by psychotherapists working with Lucy X. He chose to leak his findings to the press, believing that the police would ultimately bury or ignore his work. Whether or not one trusts Hoskins' judgement at this time in his life, it is telling that he was allowed to work on such high profile cases, given that he was obviously suffering from extreme mental distress. The total acceptance of transgender ideology within the senior ranks of the police services meant he was relied upon for his expertise at a time when he clearly needed help.

Hoskins continues to write for various publications, including the *Mail on Sunday*, and has clarified his position on transgenderism and the NHS, taking a moderately 'gender-critical' stance. It's hard not to see his life as ultimately tragic, a man broken by the Congo and haunted by the spiritual world of its inhabitants. Death, the suffering of children, witchcraft, ritual sacrifice - these themes have attached themselves to him ever since he refused to perform the rites to save his child. Despite this, he has struggled and persevered to help bring an end to the scourge of modern witchcraft accusations and deaths, particularly in Britain, and has relentlessly pointed out the failings of a world with open borders, where children can be trafficked and tortured with impunity. No doubt he will find himself on the front lines of this battle again as cases of witchcraft continue to grow in England. He has never shaken whatever attached itself to him all those years in the jungles of central Africa, but maybe this is how some curses work, a man must suffer to see what he is made of, and what he might do with his life. ◩

Stone Age Herbalist tweets @paracelsus1092. For links to all of his writing and podcast appearances, visit linktr.ee/stoneageherbalist. A collection of his essays, Berserkers, Cannibals and Shamans, *is available now via Amazon.*

TILTING AT BLACKPILLS

essay **BY RAW EGG NATIONALIST**

In this polemical essay, RAW EGG NATIONALIST asks what it really means to be a "blackpilled" writer. Are "dissident right" writers too gloomy for their own good? And, more importantly, what is a "dissident right" writer in the first place?

In Michel Houllebecq's novel *Platform*, Michel Renault, a bored civil servant who has just come into a substantial inheritance from his father, meets an enigmatic woman, Valérie, while visiting Thailand as a sex tourist. Back in France, they begin an affair which escalates into ever more dangerous and exhibitionist forms of sex – S&M, swinging, and public encounters. Michel quits his job, and tries to help Valérie and her boss rescue their failing travel business through a series of sex-tourism packages marketed at wealthy Western tourists. Eventually, the three travel to Thailand on one of these new packages. As they laze on sun loungers, and Michel begins to feel reconciled to his new life of tropical hedonism, events take an unexpected, and deadly, swerve.

"Just as I turned to give Valérie another grateful look, I heard a sort of click to my right. Then I noticed an engine noise coming from the sea, which cut out immediately. At the front of the terrace, a tall blonde woman stood up, screaming. Then came the first burst of gunfire, a brief crackle. She turned towards us, bringing her hands up to her face: a bullet had hit her in the eye, the socket was now no more than a bloody hole; then she collapsed without a sound. Then I saw our assailants, three men wearing turbans, moving swiftly in our direction, machine-guns in hand."

The terrorist attack leaves Valérie and many others dead, destroying Michel's dream of perpetual sex on the beach. After convalescing in a psychiatric hospital in Paris, he returns to Thailand to commit suicide – revealing, finally, that the novel has been his lengthy suicide note to the reader.

Platform is notable for a number of reasons. Besides propelling Houellebecq into the leagues of literary superstardom – the very opposite of the dreaded sophomore slump – and winning him a high-profile religious-hatred trial (acquitted), the novel began a tradition of eerie prescience in Houellebecq's work which has continued to this day. *Platform* was published on 27 August 2001, less than two weeks before the Islamic terror attacks of September 11, and the specific style of attack Houellebecq describes in the novel bears a close similarity to the Bali bombings that took place a little over a year later. An even more stunning coincidence attended the release of his second "Islam novel" 13 years later. *Submis-*

sion, which imagines the capitulation of the French elite to aggressive political Islam, was released on 7 January 2015, the very day of the Charlie Hebdo massacre in Paris. But wait – there's more. The follow-up, *Serotonin*, with its theme of a violent uprising among French farmers, closely foreshadowed the Gilets Jaune movement, which convulsed France until the pandemic brought it to a swift end. Clearly, Houellebecq is in touch with something.

For my purposes, however, *Platform* is notable because it reveals a rather more complicated Houellebecq than we might otherwise be led to expect. Houellebecq, we are told, is the king of the depressing novel – the novel without hope, the novel of life, ultimately, without meaning. Through the lives of unlikeable, maladjusted men, the emptiness of modern Western existence – the *inescapable* emptiness – is revealed in unflinching detail. These are the real, bitter, fruits of the global triumph of liberalism. Houellebecq is the novelist of the End of History. He's the incel bard (although he is, actually, married to a much younger woman – Japanese, I think). Houellebecq is "blackpilled" – if by "blackpilled" you mean "an extreme nihilist", which not everybody who uses the term does, as we'll see.

Except Houellebecq isn't. "Blackpilled", I mean. Rather than the End of History – a flat space outside meaningful time – what *Platform* gives us instead is the shocking, violent *return* of History. The terrible, but also terribly exciting, return of contingency to a world which promised only minor ameliorations until the universe finally collapsed in on itself, billions of years in the future. (And don't forget how spectacularly life imitated art just a week or so after the book's release.)

Rather than being a novel of despair, *Platform* is a novel of great hope – or, at least, that's how I read it anyway. This is the message: life is not forever destined to be a succession of pleasant, but nonetheless meaningless, sex acts (for those who are lucky enough to get them, of course) until one expires – in flagrante, perhaps, with a nubile young Thai masseuse. No, life might also be a violent death at the hands of a jet-ski-riding jihadi, or something else equally unforeseen. Possibilities!

For Michel Renault, however, the attack and the death of his lover Valérie is the final straw; and the broader implication, developed further in *Submission*, is that the West is too tired and corrupt to shed its heavy skin. Only an outside force, like an aggressive religion spreading through immigration and demographic change, can transform the old order.

Be that as it may, there are plenty of other indications throughout Houellebecq's oeuvre – chinks of light, if you will – that reveal that all is not darkness and despair in his world. All we need is the eyes to see them.

It's for this reason, and others, that I was surprised to see Houellebecq labelled the master of a "blackpilled" aesthetic that's supposedly dominant among young "right-leaning" fiction writers today. In his essay, "Overdosing on the Literary Black-pill", one of the centrepieces of the IM-1776 *Art and Literature for Dissidents* pamphlet, Alex Perez makes two claims about these "dissident" writers: i) that they are simply aping Houellebecq, but lack the necessary personal charm and writerly skills to do so in a way that is anything other than repel-lent to most readers; and ii) that if a proper literary movement is to emerge among the "dissident right", these young writers must find a way to look outside themselves and reach a broader audience of "well-adjusted people".

I don't disagree with the broad thrust of this diagnosis, if the broad thrust is that there are some bad writers on this side of the internet, because there clearly are. The worst of their writing is very bad – derivative, charmless, pointless. And yes, some of it does look like a bad impression of Houellebecq circa his first and most incel-y novel, *Whatever*. Imitation may indeed be the sincerest form of flattery, but it seldom makes for great reading. And this is true even in the case of someone who really can write, like Cormac McCarthy. His early Faulkner impressions, especially the anti-picaresque *Suttree*, are pretty tough going, no substitute for the real thing. An obvious part of the problem is, as Perez suggests, that anybody can publish their writing on the internet now, without any real form of quality control. (I won't get in to the bad poetry here, much of which suffers from the mistake of thinking that we can just forget the twentieth century – i.e. modernism in its various forms – and go back to writing sonnets and heroic poetry like nothing happened. We can't.)

That being said, it's also plain as day that there's a huge amount of great fiction being written by "dissident" or "right-leaning" authors, whatever you choose to call them. Some of it has been featured in this magazine. Zero HP Lovecraft's uncanny corporate nightmares ("Dagon"). Faisal Marzipan's blackly comedic reimagining of an interview for a top consultancy firm ("The Minnetonka Safe Haven Project"). Detective Wolfman's archetypal adventures ("Heartsfire"). Or what about "The Scrimshander", one of many gems in the last issue? Or "human.exe" from this issue? Not one of these stories displays any of the defects Perez identifies. Instead we have daring imagination, originality, horror, suspense, excitement, craft, as well as considerable charm and wit. These are stories that could – and should – reach the widest possible audiences. In no way is it obvious

to me, then, that this "blackpilled" genre is the dominant trend. It might be *a* trend, but it doesn't strike me as something we should be unduly worried about.

And for the bad writing Perez identifies, I'm not even sure it's Houellebecq who's most to blame. Brett Easton Ellis is a very obvious influence on that kind of writing – I've handled more than a few Bateman monologues as editor of this magazine ("Then I apply a JOOV 600nm red light to my testicles for 10 minutes while I prepare the rest of my routine…") – and there's also Chuck Pahlaniuk, author of *Fight Club*, to name just two.

Where the analysis really starts to fall apart, though, is when we consider what it really means to be a "blackpilled" writer, according to Perez. He doesn't actually give a definition, but we can cobble one together easily enough. "Blackpilled" writing is full of "world-weariness" and "doom and gloom". It's written by and appeals to "depressives". Okay: so far, so uncontroversial. But then we're told these writers are also playing at being "angry young men", which rather cuts against the grain of the general apathy and indifference we tend to associate with having swallowed and digested the black pill. "Blackpilled" writing is also "base" (not "based"), full of "repulsiveness", "debased and debauched" and "antisocial" – things we needn't associate, on their own or even in combination, with being "blackpilled".

It's not just that the implicit definition is a little bit confused. It's that it's somehow capacious enough to include a writer who is so obviously not "blackpilled" that I find myself wondering what Perez is really up to here. I'm talking, believe it or not, about Bronze Age Pervert. BAP is, of course, an enormous influence on writers of every stripe on this side of the internet, and I'm sure that many of the writers who write the bad Bateman monologues have read *Bronze Age Mindset* and no doubt love it. But do I really need to say that this means practically nothing about BAP himself? Calling BAP "blackpilled" because of one tiny segment of his audience is about as meaningful as saying that, because I'm currently listening to "Easy Lover" on repeat, Phil Collins is a "dissident right" singer. Hardly.

BAP's message is the absolute opposite of "blackpilled". It feels ridiculous even to have to say this. And yet, here I am, saying it. The positivity of the book is one of the main reasons it's been so popular. Yes, we live in a trash world, a world of owned space where the young and vital are subject to a stultifying gynocracy; yes the current order is antithetical to higher forms of life; yes you feel trapped, hemmed in, circumscribed, put out to pasture – but things were this way once before and they changed radically, and now there are already signs of another radical change on the horizon. BAP isn't just offering a diagnosis of the ills of the modern world, he's very clearly pointing us towards the exit and giving us a slap on the back for good measure; although, as Perez notes, perceptively, *Bronze Age Mindset* isn't a self-help book. If it's *Lift, Love, Laugh* you want, you'll have to wait for my next book (I've got dibs on that title, by the way, so hands off!).

But Perez doesn't want you to pay attention to the message of *Bronze Age Mindset*. This, I think, is where the true purpose of the essay is revealed. I'll let Perez speak for himself now:

"*BAM* is certainly a 'blackpilled text', but the driving force behind the book is not the content, but the… chaotic energy that permeates it, which is what young writers should be taking away from it. What a book says stylistically and aesthetically is often of greater import than whatever thematic point of view it's trying – and often failing – to propagate."

So what you're saying is… the famous BAP patois is what really matters about *Bronze Age Mindset*? Ignore the content: it's just a vehicle for BAP to break the rules of strict grammar and coin some funny new slang words? As much as it may be true that BAP-speak has become ubiquitous among little (and even large) frog accounts, this is well and truly ass-backwards. Of course Perez is welcome to dislike *Bronze Age Mindset*. But to suggest that the "driving force behind the book", the reason why it's become a subject of feverish excitement everywhere from Twitter to the corridors of the White House, is not the actual themes of the work, but the energy, style and aesthetic – as if, in any case, form and content could be separated in such a way here – seems, frankly, bizarre.

At last, then, I think we can see what the "blackpilled" epithet really amounts to. Rather than being a criticism of a genuine identifiable movement, it's just a tag for things the author doesn't like, and one of those things is clearly *Bronze Age Mindset*.

Now, before you interject that this laddy doth protest too much, let me say that I don't think the attempt to minimise the message or enduring impact of *Bronze Age Mindset* is confined to just this essay. In actual fact, I see this as a broader phenomenon. There are plenty who have been happy to ride the BAP wave and be associated with him – at a safe distance – but who have never believed a word of what he says in *Bronze Age Mindset*. This became abundantly clear after BAP's most recent banning from Twitter last year, when many accounts that had reaped the benefits of his largesse turned on him the moment he was gone. Despite the book's incontrovertible importance, it's just too extreme, too off-the-wall – nowhere near "respectable" enough for those "dissidents" who are merely waiting for the door to be opened, at long last, to let them in to the establisment party. *Finally, we've arrived!* Seen in this light, Perez's use of words like "base", "debased and debauched" and "anti-social", but especially his injunction for "blackpilled" writers to appeal to "well-adjusted people", looks rather more telling. So too does his insistence on referring to *Bronze Age Mindset* as "the most popular *self-published book* [my emphasis] among the blackpilled writers". This can only be a deliberate slight against a book which has sold tens of thousands of copies, consistently outselling the most "popular" astroturfed writers in fields like ancient history, the classics and philosophy. As far as white pills go, I'd say those sale figures are a pretty big one, wouldn't you?

Of course, this would hardly be the first time that "dangerous" thinkers have been neutered by those of a more – how shall we say? – mainstream inclination. (Note: I'm not saying that a mainstream influence is something we shouldn't be trying to cultivate, especially since we already have a pretty significant one.) Nietzsche is an obvious example here. I don't mean how his sister, Elisabeth Förster-Nietzsche, selectively edited his work the better to fit with her own ideological commitments. Rather, I mean the way that French postmodernists like Deleuze, Derrida and Foucault focused on his style and method ("genealogy") at the expense of the substance of what he actually said. This gave us the largely unrecognisable "New Nietzsche", as well as absurdities like the "Nietzschean" Foucault, as fitting a candidate for the Last Man as you could hope to find: a bald, bespectacled boy-lover who found nirvana spreading HIV in the bath-houses of San Francisco. No less absurd is the "liberal" Nietzsche of Bernard Williams, a sort of Humean sceptic who, by an extreme act of leg-crossing, can be made to sit nicely among the grave philosophers of the Anglo-American analytic tradition. Pffffft.

In all honesty, though, I think BAP will continue to speak to readers on his own terms, long after most of his current interpreters and critics have vanished from sight.

What remains of Perez's essay is an attempt to provide positive advice for how the "blackpilled" writers can build a movement that will gain wider recognition. Building a movement, especially a political movement, brings its own problems. One of the most fundamental issues is one that dogs all explicitly political art: Is the art's defining feature its political message? If so, what is that message? What makes an artist a "dissident right" artist, as opposed to something else?

Wouldn't it be more sensible for the aim to be to make good art, first and foremost? After all, by their own admission, most artists have deliberately abandoned the traditional principles of aesthetics (representation, harmony, conformity with nature, etc.), leaving artists on the right with a totally open goal. Being able to depoliticise the issue – to say that artists on the right are simply doing art – could also be an advantage in certain situations. This would be my suggestion, or the beginning of one, but it needs development, and here is not the place to do that.

These and many more questions remain to be resolved at present. But if there's one thing I know already, it's that the "dissident right" won't win any battles by tilting at imaginary enemies – or by biting the hand that has so generously fed it.

Raw Egg Nationalist's new book The Eggs Benedict Option, *is out now.*

Albrecht Dürer, *Knight, Death and the Devil* (1513)

TRADITION

translation **BY MARTIN**

MARTIN gives us an exclusive new translation of an early essay by Ernst Jünger. What is the real meaning of "tradition", and how do we act in the interest of the future while following its dictates?

Tradition — is a noble and proud word for a race that has the will to put the emphasis back on the side of blood. The individual does not dwell alone in a physical place, but as a member of a community, for which he has to live and, if necessary, to sacrifice himself. That is a realization which probably every man who has a sense of responsibility possesses and defends - in his own particular way and with his own particular means. But the individual is bound not only to a higher community in space, but also in an even more significant, though invisible, way in time. A father's blood pulses through one's own, he lives on in realms and bonds that they have created, preserved and defended. Created, preserved and defended, so that he might take the work from their fist into his own and manage it worthily. The man of the present is the center between the past and the future. Life shoots like the glowing spark of a fuse through the bond of the sexes, it burns them out and, nevertheless, establishes a connection which goes from the beginning to the end. Soon the man of the present will also be a has-been, but the thought gives him peace and security that his work and his deeds do not perish with him, but that they have laid the foundation on which the future man, the heir, stands with weapons and tools.

That which makes an action historical: that it is not in itself and is not done for itself, but that it is structured into a meaningful action, that it is directed by the deeds of one's forefathers and aimed into the mysterious realm of the unborn. It is dark on this side and on the other side of the deed, its roots disappear in the gray of the past, its fruits fall into the land of inheritance, which the deed will never see, and yet it is determined and preserved from both sides, and therein lies its timeless splendor and its highest glory.

This is what distinguishes the hero and the warrior from the countryman and the adventurer, that he draws his strength from higher reserves than from his personal ones, and that the glowing beacon of his deed is not a flickering fire, but the blazing fire in which the future is forged around the past. In the greatness of the adventurer there is something accidental, a wild incursion into colorful landscapes, which also has its beauty, but in the hero the necessary, fate-conditioned is completed, he is the uniquely moral man, who is significant not only in himself, not only today, but also for all and for any time.

On whatever battlefield and at whatever seemingly lost post - where a past is to be preserved and fought for a future, no deed can be lost. The individual can certainly be lost, but his destiny, his happiness and his perfection is a downfall for a higher, further goal. The man without ties dies and with him his work, because it was tailored in its dimensions only to himself; the hero perishes, but his demise is like the blood-red setting of the sun, which promises a new and more beautiful tomorrow. In the same way, we must remember the great war as a glowing sunset, in the colors of which a glorious tomorrow is already determined. So we must think of our fallen friends, and recognize in their demise the sign of completion, the sharpest affirmation of life itself. Far as from disgusting filth, we must refrain from the evaluation of the Kramerseele "that it was all in vain," if we want to find our happiness in living in the space of destiny and flowing in the mysterious stream of blood, if we want to work in a meaningful, significant landscape, and not vegetate in a time and space in which we have been placed by the accident of birth.

No, birth must not be an accident for us! It is the act that immerses us in our actual earthly realm, and that determines, with a thousand symbolic threads, our place in the life-world. Through it we become members of the nation, the community of those bound by birth. From here we enter life, from a fixed point, but in a movement that began long before us and will end late after us. We are passing through only one section of this vast trajectory, but over this section we must not only carry a full inheritance, but be equal to all the demands of time.

Now, vile minds, debauched in the squalor of our great cities, come up with the wisdom that our birth was a game of chance, and that "we could just as well have been born French as Germans." Of course, for the one who thinks like that, it is true. He is an accidental man. The happiness that lies in feeling born with necessity into a great destiny, in feeling its tensions and struggles as one's own, and in rising - or sinking - with it, is foreign to him.

These brains always come out when misfortune weighs on the communities united by birth, and this is characteristic for them. (We should briefly point out the last, very skilful move of the intellect to parasitically and destructively penetrate into the community of blood and to distort its essence intellectually, namely by the term "community of fate", which at first sight seems to be quite appropriate. But the community of destiny also includes a negro who was taken by surprise at the beginning of the war in Germany, who was drawn into our path of suffering from bread to root vegetables. A "community of destiny" in this sense is formed by the passengers of a sinking steamer, in contrast to the community of blood of the crew of a warship sinking with the flag flying).

The national man values being born into a firmly defined boundary, indeed he sees in it his highest pride. When he transcends his borders, he does so not by flowing formlessly beyond them, but by extending them into the future and into the past. Its strength rests in the fact that it possesses direction, and with it a more instinctive security, an orientation from the ground up, which is given to the blood, and which does not need the fluctuating and changing signal lanterns of sophisticated concepts. Thus life grows into a greater unity, and thus it becomes itself a unity by being meaningfully bound in each of its moments.

Sharply delineated by its boundaries, by sacred rivers, fearsome mountains and vast seas, the life of a national race fixes itself in space. Based on a tradition and directed towards a distant future, it is fixed in time. Woe to him who cuts off his own roots, he becomes an impotent, a parasitic man. To deny the past is also to deny the future, and to perish with the volatile waves of the present.

But for the nationalist there is an equally great danger, that is that he forgets the present. Having tradition implies the duty to live out this tradition. The nation is not a house on which each generation, like a generation of coral, only has to add a new story, or in whose space, set once and for all, it only has to exist in a bad way. A castle, a solidly built suburban house, seems to be set once and for all after its completion. But soon a new generation, out of new needs, sees the necessity of important changes. Or it burns down, it is destroyed, and a new, different building rises above the old foundation walls. The facades change, every stone is replaced, and yet, in a very special sense, it remains the same house. Was it the perfect house only in the Renaissance or in the Baroque, did it have then a style that is valid forever? No, but what it was then is somehow hidden in what it is today.

Today it is perhaps coolly structured as an expression of a feeling in values of the highest, active energy, but this expression is only conceivable on the layered ground of a tradition. In every line and in every scale, the past mysteriously resonates, and yet it is the present that determines the face of the whole, so that it lifts us up, carries us away in the feeling: this is us, this is ourselves! And so it must be.

So also the blood of the individual is mixed from a thousand dark bloodstreams, and yet the individual is not only the sum of his ancestors, not only the bearer of their will and qualities, but also in distinct, bounded peculiarity - he is he himself. And the same is the case with the most compre-

hensive form of the nation, with the state. Yesterday we had an empire, today we have a republic, tomorrow perhaps another empire, and the day after tomorrow a dictatorship. Each of these structures, as an invisible inheritance, more or less hidden under its formal language, also carries the content of the former, but each has the duty to be completely itself, because only in this way the full utilization of the power is achieved.

This is true also in this exact minute for every one of us. To be an heir is not to be an imitator. And to live in a tradition does not mean to limit oneself to this tradition. To inherit a house means to take care of it, but not to make a museum out of it, in which the ancestral home stands untouched. "His Kingdom [Reich] is for ever," said Luther, who laid the axe to the building of a church; he knew that a kingdom and a building, a power and its temporal expression are not the same.

"His Kingdom is for ever" — so too for us, and in this will to the essential lies our real tradition, for which one can stand up just as sharply under the roof of a republic as under that of an empire. The important thing is that the great current of blood forces all the resources and institutions of the time into its service. Whether you fight a battle with the methods of a republic or with those of a board of directors, it amounts to the same thing - if only you win it. In the age of the cold steel one must know how to win with the sword, in the age of the machine with machine guns, tanks, bomb squadrons and gas attacks. In a patrimonial age, an army must believe in fighting for its king and lord; in an age of the masses, it may desire to go to the death for any progress of a social or economic nature. Always his ideas, his faith and his morality will shimmer, yes, must shimmer, in the colorful reflections of temporal illumination, but what matters is not his insights, questions and apparent goals, but that all his power be realized within the framework of the "kingdom."

This realization is also our duty. We, too, must try to put the tremendous, bound energy of the modern state at the service of the empire, to wrest it from the clutches of the rational intellect, and to subject it to the laws of blood down to the last fly-wheel, the last bit of iron. Only then will we live tradition. We are still far from it. It is precisely the emphasis on the external form of tradition, which is characteristic of the national youth of today, that is a sign of a lack of inner strength. We do not live in museums, but in an active, hostile world. It is not a living tradition that old Fritz is painted on every cigar box, and that every ashtray and every pair of trousers receives its black-and-white bread stamp. This is advertising in the worst sense, just as the majority of our parades, commemorations and honorary days are only the most taste-less advertising, cast-iron kitsch, through which one gains nothing but followers.

Prepare yourselves for a new Rossbach in the most characteristic formations of our time, then the old one up there will be most pleased. Do not write Frederick novels, but the national novel of our time, whose material is as multifarious as life itself before your eyes. Do not live as dreamers in sunken times, but try to give the Republic clout and power directed by the current of blood, or smash it in two if it does not want to become tough. Do not reminisce about the cane of Frederick William II, which was essential in his time, but recognize that such methods of social control depend on the times, and that today it is essential to find a solution that will include the worker in the national front, as has already been done in other countries.

Be fully who you are; then you will be living both the future and the past in the fiery focus of the present and in your own deeds. Then you will have real, living tra-dition and not only its flickering reflection that can be placed in any suburban cinema.

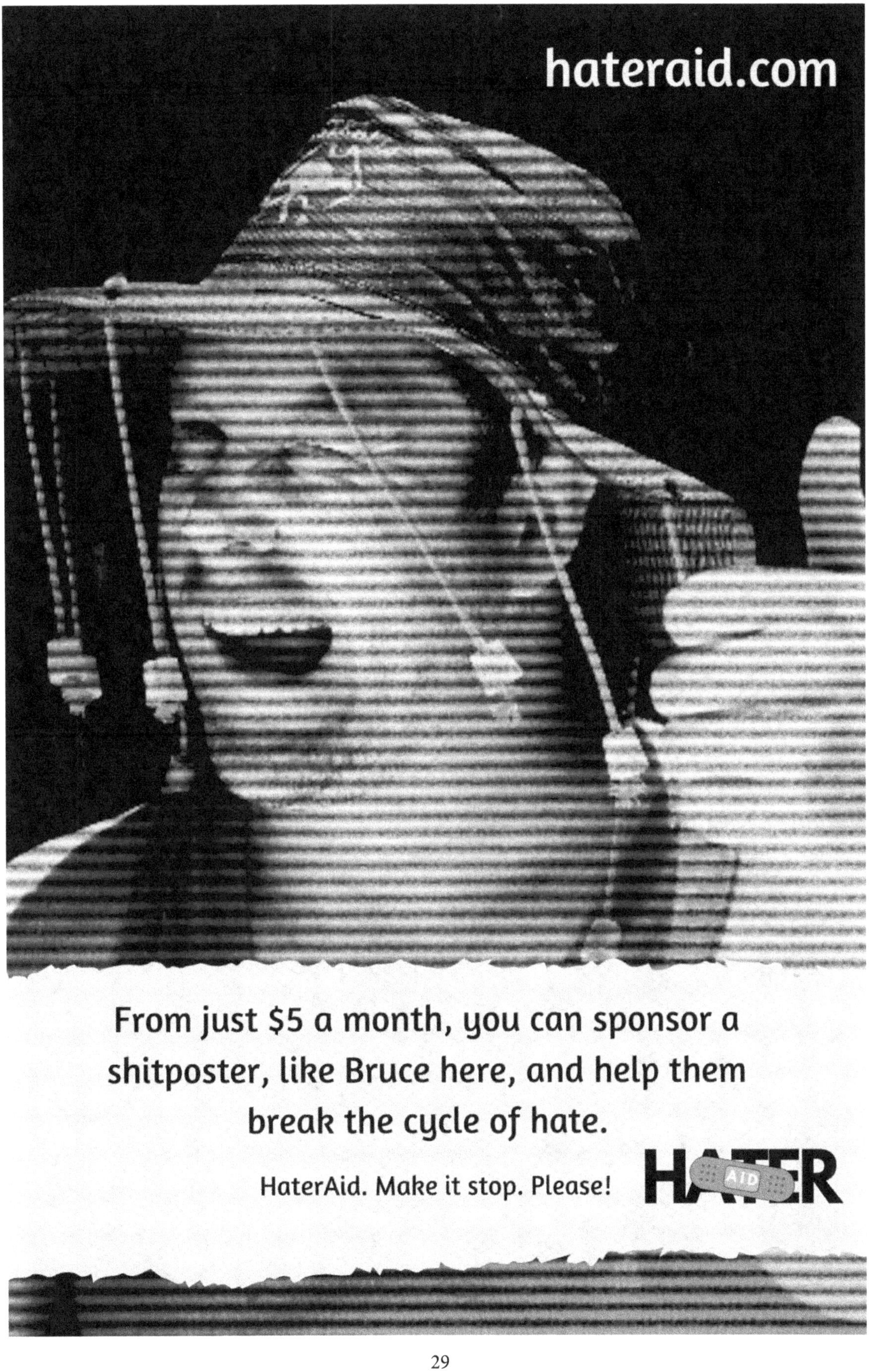
hateraid.com
From just $5 a month, you can sponsor a shitposter, like Bruce here, and help them break the cycle of hate.
HaterAid. Make it stop. Please!
HATER AID

WINNING THE CULTURE WAR

essay **BY HOSTUS**

With all this talk of hobbits and dark elves, is the culture war actually winnable for the little man? Absolutely, says HOSTUS.

Andrew Breitbart famously counselled conservatives in the US that politics are downstream of culture. He was wrong: politics and culture cannot be meaningfully distinguished. Especially when the stakes are existential, as they now are.

This error in thinking isn't the fault of the late Mr Breitbart — it's simply an error of accepting the technocratic frame. The belief that "social", "economic", or "foreign" policies can be chosen from a menu and applied to the real world. As though they were RPG stat modifiers without any second order effects or consequences.

In reality, you get exactly the culture which "policy" sees fit to subsidise. Epidemic levels of single motherhood, black girl magic in the cockpits of airliners, DEI statements as a requirement of admission to university PhD programs, Drag Queen Story Time, PrEP for dogs — and anything that materially or spiritually resembles these things — are all cultural features made possible through political agitation. You can't "just get the economy right" or "just get law and order right" when both the economy and the law have been hi-jacked to support the cultural programs of your enemy.

A turn towards the apolitical has been a defining factor of the "mainstream" right's retreat into the margins for as long as most of us have been alive. We are all aware of this, but we should take great pains to remember it — this is a losing strategy. It always will be. Indeed, the only circumstances under which anyone would cede such large amounts of territory in the first place are those of complete hopelessness.

Every victory is, by definition, the counterpart to a defeat. And the only possible path to "victory" for us implies that our Weltanschauung prevails entirely over that of the massed and greasy bugman armies of the other side.

Even if you have already acknowledged this fact intellectually, it probably still feels like a daunting prospect. Total victory doesn't seem very likely where we are now. But before you surrender to despair, I'd like you to consider something very important. To win, you only have to convince 5%.

The past few years — and in particular, COVID — have one central lesson for the man willing to learn it: most people are culturally, politically, morally, and socially inert. The NPC meme is a genuine and true statement about reality.

The overwhelming majority of the population has no substantive views of its own.

It simply regards the current "consensus" as correct. If it's what everyone else thinks, it must be right. If it's currently law, it must be moral. They enquire no further than this.

Fortunately for you, they don't need to. If the "consensus" changes, they'll happily believe whatever it changes into. "Free minds" are the only element you need to persuade, and these are remarkably thin on the ground. I said 5% above. In reality, the number is likely much smaller. But even a fraction of this small number will be more than enough to get the job done.

With all that said, winning might be simple, but it certainly won't be easy. "Our" sphere, whatever you might like to call it, is still in its political infancy. The final victory might take decades of work to achieve, and we would be foolish not to expect tactical victories and defeats to occur along the way.

I want to say all of this in the hope that it will provide some encouragement and morale. At the moment, visible victories are few and far between. But I also want to warn you against a very specific type of demoralisation. And to do that, we unfortunately need to talk about hobbits.

Curtis Yarvin's recent pronouncements on the issue of the culture war (framed as a conflict between hobbits and elves) put on full display one of the most consistent errors in his epistemology: he is an elitist who has a very confused idea as to the nature of power in human societies.

His hobbit/elf schema (which is really only a loose re-skin of the vaishiya/brahmin or morlock/eloi dichotomy he used years ago while writing Unqualified Reservations) does get one self-evident thing right: there is a segment of the population which is both unfit to rule, and for the most part has no interest in ruling.

Where his analysis fails is in his characterisation of the bounds of this group, and his definition of the other side of the coin, those who can rule.

Yarvin's "elves", by his own definitions, constitute an enormous group which at its greatest extent includes anyone who has ever graduated from some form of tertiary education. His most recent definition, "[those who have] fully entered modernity, [those] who live for self actualisation" is actually even more extreme, and almost precludes the existence of "hobbits" at all.

There is not a single person in any western country who has not "fully entered modernity". Not even the Amish can really make this claim. "Self actualisation", for its part, is a concept that's been in circulation for over 100 years, and in its academic conception is taken to be a goal towards which all humans strive innately. In spiritual terms, it is the drive to telos. In material terms, it is the drive to most fully express one's genetic programming. It cannot, therefore, be the province of any one social group.

Or, to put it another way, the hobbit at his grill is fully self actualised according to his own potential and temperament.

What Yarvin is in fact driving at is a basic distinction of character and spirit that might very well be a difference in basic biology. Most people simply do not have the intelligence, motivation, resources, or organisational capacity to rule themselves or anyone else. However, almost none of these people are in Yarvin's audience.

In fact many of these people fall under the umbrella of Yarvin's "elves". Most "elves" are not political, social, or cultural taste-makers, they are exactly as inert in these spheres as Yarvin believes hobbits to be.

The average state department or pentagon officer, the average college professor — to say nothing of the average college graduate — has no power whatsoever. They might be able to exercise power as the temporary deputies of those who do —provided they act according to their interests — but this is not the same as being in power, or holding power oneself.

A pawn is not a player. When the culture war is eventually won, most of Yarvin's "elves" will be nowhere to be found, because their convictions are not their own. They are the echo of the consensus, and they will just as eagerly echo the new consensus.

For all the trails they have blazed, the main flaw of Yarvin and his ilk is a tendency towards overcomplication. None of our present problems are unsolvable. None of our present enemies are beyond defeat. Perhaps most importantly, the "structure" of our system doesn't actually matter that much. The system is simply whatever the current ruling elite — the shapers of the culture —d esire it to be.

None of this is beyond change, but that change is not going to come from shadowy cadres of Yarvinite "dark elves".

(As a brief parenthetical: by Yarvin's own definition of what a "dark elf" is, an elf sympathetic to hobbit ends, isn't the very event he's describing as a hollow victory a textbook example of a dark elf op? His argument defeats itself.)

I believe the change will come from you. If you are reading this, the chances are you are fortunate enough to be one of the small portion of the population capable of genuine independent thought. Congratulations. It will be your privilege to suffer and triumph in the creation of a new culture.

By this I don't simply mean through the means of the arts; although the arts are an excellent vehicle for this as we've seen. The culture that will ultimately "win" the war is still in its infancy, forming slowly and haltingly, as a product of all of the actions we are choosing to take right now. I don't know exactly what form it will take, but neither does Yarvin, and nor does anyone else. But what I do know is that it will be wholly unlike anything what has come before it. You may yet live to see man-made wonders beyond your aspirations.

IN CONVERSATION WITH...

interview **BY NOOR BIN LADIN**

NOOR BIN LADIN interviews RAW EGG NATIONALIST about his new book, *THE EGGS BENEDICT OPTION*, for which she wrote an exclusive preface.

For readers of MAN'S WORLD, my guest for this issue needs no introduction. You'll most definitely be familiar with REN's work, and beyond that, his life's mission educating us all on the benefits of raw eggs, good health, masculinity and much more. A true renaissance man of our times, the list of topics REN can discuss at length is long! That being said, for this issue we thought it would be fitting to have a conversation about his new book, The Eggs Benedict Option (for which I had the honour of writing the foreword).

In one sentence, The Eggs Benedict Option *is the antidote to the Great Reset.* In the book, REN meticulously outlines the Globalists' efforts over decades to capture one of the most essential resources necessary for our survival and endurance: our food. Due to their success in controlling what we eat — and with it the success of deliberately downgrading its quality and advocating poor diet recommendations — our society has declined dramatically compared to the early 20th century. REN documents the factors and methods deployed that have led to a multitude of negative consequences, all undeniable: we suffer of weaker physiognomies, degenerative diseases, downgraded DNA, and decreased fertility, among many other ailments, largely because of the "food" we consume.

While it is painful to take stock of the results caused by the modern Western diet, there is hope, and it lies in The Eggs Benedict Option. The book shows us a way out of this hell they have planned for us — live in the pod, eat the bugs — by reclaiming the way we produce and consume our food. Household gardening and regenerative agriculture, practiced in widespread fashion by our ancestors but also in our recent past and in certain parts of the world today, can once again become the norm — a "New Normal" that actually benefits us. Solutions are out there and have been proven to not only work, but to replenish our soils as well, which have been stripped for decades since the advent of industrialized agriculture. The field of regenerative agriculture is fascinating, and The Eggs Benedict Option offers a great introduction to an essential part of reclaiming our autonomy from the Globalists.

The book is a must read, so get your copy as soon as you can — and in the meantime, let's find out more from the author himself.

REN, you've been at the forefront of denouncing impoverished diets and the var-

ious poisonous chemicals that are found in our food, pushing instead for clean, nutritious eating habits. Tell us how the book came about, and what was the main takeaway you wanted to convey.

This will make you laugh. I had this old partially read copy of *The Benedict Option* [by Rod Dreher] kicking around on the floor, getting progressively more and more scuffed. Anyway, one day I looked across at it – I may have been sitting on the loo at the time – and all of a sudden it hit me. THE EGGS BENEDICT OPTION! Well, now I had a great name. But what to do with it?

Initially I thought I'd just write an essay about *The Benedict Option* and what I saw as the problem with the general thesis of the book (that it's predicated on the idea that intentional Christian communities will simply be left alone by their avowed enemies to do their own thing, which doesn't seem at all realistic to me). But then I thought, "the Eggs Benedict Option" is too good to waste on a short essay, so I decided it would have to be a book. I started riffing on the idea of a Benedict Option for RWBBs [right-wing bodybuilders) and what that might look like.

It quickly became clear to me that it would have to be about the Great Reset and the food transformation that the globalists have in store for us, something I had been following closely already. And since *The Benedict Option* lays out a positive vision for how Christians can respond to the increasingly hostile culture around them, I wanted to do the same. I didn't just want the book to be a description of all the bad things the globalists want to do. That would be extremely depressing – a black pill. So I needed a comprehensive plan to fight back.

Fortunately, I didn't have to look too far, since I had been reading a lot about regenerative agriculture. I've long been of the opinion that small-scale food production is the answer to so many of our current problems and I'd just been turned on, thanks to the *Small Farmer's Journal*, to the little known (in the West at least), but extremely important, form of agriculture known as "Russian household gardening" or "dacha gardening". This became the jumping-off point, then, for a plan to fight the globalist vision of the future of food with a renewed localism, at the social and political level.

If the book has a main takeaway, it's that although the powers that oppose us are great, their victory is by no means assured. Klaus Schwab is right about one thing: this is the perfect opportunity for fundamental change. It's just a question of whose vision of the future wins. Ours must prevail!

I think what most people fail to comprehend, is that all of this was deliberate. What makes the EBO so compelling – and convincing for those new to this theme – is that you only referred to official statements from the Globalists' mouths, demonstrating their machinations are indeed intentional.

Yes, exactly. This is something that greatly frustrates me when people start talking about the Great Reset. They start with a document like "Welcome to 2030", the famous "thinkpiece" from 2016 that provoked so much discussion and revulsion, and very quickly end up talking about ancient bloodlines and other stuff that just makes them look, to your man on the street, like a total crank. This is very bad. It's a distraction and it discredits everybody. Our opponents can simply say, "Look at these people. They're insane with all their talk of lizard people etc."

I mean, there are all sorts of understandable reasons why people let speculation get the better of reason when they talk about the Great Reset, not least of all because the World Economic Forum has a knack for the kind of stunning coincidences that would shock even the most tired of conspiracists back into life. Just look at Event 201, the pandemic planning exercise held in October 2019 that basically predicted every aspect of the coming pandemic, including the unheralded social restrictions that were imposed. My friend Eugyppius wrote very perceptively about this in Issue Four. It's mind-boggling. But it's also hard to get anywhere further than that initial jolt. Event 201 might incline you to think that the pandemic was, to some degree even if not entirely, a plandemic, but there's just no way to bridge the gap, as it were – in exactly the same way as, however strange it might seem that three prominent opponents of the creation of the Federal Reserve just so happened to die on the Titanic, there's no way to get from that fact to a credible argument that the Titanic was deliberately sunk to ensure its creation. I talk about this kind of stuff in my Meditations essay for this issue of the magazine, and ask why we care so much about who or what Klaus Schwab actually is. That kind of talk adds nothing to what we already know.

And we already know a huge amount. There are books and articles and studies and public pronouncements, going back years, laying out exactly what the globalists want to do to the food supply and why. It's all there – publicly accessible – and just waiting to be given a proper airing. People think "You vill eat ze bugs!", but actually there's an entire detailed plan for a global diet that's been produced by one of the

World Economic Forum's partners, the EAT Foundation. This "Planetary Health Diet" is a more or less entirely plant-based diet, developed in order to feed a projected world population of 10 billion in a way that is "healthy" (according to their perverted standards) and that allows the governments of the world to meet their climate targets. Everything you need to know about this project – who is involved and how, what they want to do and why – is there, ready to be discovered. If my book serves any purpose, I hope at least it will make people realise how far advanced the globalist plan is, and of course how bad it is too.

So we don't need to speculate about Klaus Schwab's links to the Third Reich's nuclear programme or whether Justin Trudeau and Jacinda Arden were created in a lab. The globalists want to force us to change our diet in the most fundamental way, in a way that has never happened in history (although there are important parallels), and that's more than enough to get people motivated to resist the Great Reset.

One of these important parallels in your account is with the Neolithic Revolution, which you call "the original Great Reset". Control over what we eat has been a part of our rulers' playbook for a long time then? How ancient is the control of food as a form of social control?

As I say in the preface of the book, social control and control of the food supply go together like peas and carrots. We're talking about one of the most ancient, most fundamental rules of government, which has

> ## Klaus Schwab is right about one thing: this is the perfect opportunity for fundamental change. It's just a question of whose vision of the future wins

been understood by rulers for thousands of years. I wanted to make this fact unambiguously clear right at the beginning of the book.

In the preface I discuss Plato's *Republic* and the idea expressed in the second book that the perfect harmonious society must be vegetarian. Although this isn't the society that Plato's Socrates ends up elaborating for the rest of the book, it's very striking that, nevertheless, he sees a vegetarian diet as being one that will best quiet the passions and desires of ordinary people, allowing them to live peacefully, without questioning their lot. The people as happy cattle, essentially. But behind that you have a more general fact – that as early as the mid-fourth century BC philosophers clearly believed that you could fundamentally change a society by changing its diet – which is no less interesting than the specifics of what Plato says.

Now this is ancient enough – we're talking 2,500 years roughly – but in fact we can go back even further, to the Neolithic Revolution, the creation of fixed-field farming in the Near East, to see the link between changing diet and changing forms of social control revealed in the most dramatic fashion. Rather than being the happy tale of Progress we're generally told it was, the Neolithic Revolution brought terrible misery to the majority of people who were caught up in it. Only a narrow elite, who often came in from "outside", as it were, as invaders, really benefitted. And this is clear in all sorts of evidence, whether we're talking about skeletal evidence of serious malnourishment among early farmers or evidence for societal collapse, which often seems to have taken place as a result of early farmers running away at the first chance they got.

An account of the events of the Neolithic Revolution, and a comparison with the Great Reset plan for food, is central to the book, not only to reveal that societies can be fundamentally transformed by altering how food is produced and distributed, but also to reveal what is at stake in the coming food transformation. I'm in no doubt that many of the things that happened to Neolithic man when he became a farmer – the malnutrition, the shrinking, the illnesses – are likely to make an unwelcome return if we're all forced to eat plant-based diets. I mean this in all seriousness.

Weston Price is unequivocal that humans cannot reach their proper physical potential eating plant foods alone, and especially not industrially produced plant foods

Right. Your discussion of the physical changes induced by change in diet is fascinating – and scary. I highly enjoyed reading about the work of Weston Price, author of *Nutrition and Physical Degeneration*, who proved the superiority of animal vs. plant based diets. Information that would be useful for vegans...

If everybody who thought they wanted to be a vegetarian or vegan was made to read Weston Price first, only the most stubborn and deluded – sadly a decent proportion of vegans especially – would continue down that path. Another book I use quite liberally in the section on the probable health effects of the globalist plant-based diet is Lierre Keith's *The Vegetarian Myth*, which is an interesting combination of nutritional information and autobiography. Keith ruined her body by persisting in a vegan diet for nearly two decades, despite almost immediately starting to suffer from excruciating side-effects. One of the things that finally broke her – made her repent from veganism, if you will – was reading Weston Price and realising that she was essentially going against nature with her current diet. She was responsible for all of the dreadful things she was suffering, because she had chosen not to nourish herself with the foods that make human beings have perfect health – i.e. nutrient-dense animal foods. Weston Price is unequivocal that humans cannot reach their proper physical potential eating plant foods alone, and especially not industrially produced plant foods.

I should say some more about Price for those who don't know. He was a dentist in Cleveland in the late nineteenth and early twentieth centuries who noticed an alarming trend among his patients, especially the children. More and more he noticed malformed jaws – crowded teeth, cavities, narrow dental arches – that not only marred his patients' physical appearance, but also reduced their health and development and even, in some cases, led to serious behavioural problems. Price was convinced that this was due to a change in diet: this was the time that people in the Corn Belt and the rest of America started to move from a diet of natural whole foods to industrially produced food, especially grain-based products. He decided, around about the 1920s, to travel the world and put his theory to the test by seeing if he could find traditional groups of people who displayed perfect dentition and learn what they were eating. So he travelled the length and breadth of the world over a period of years, from North America to the Torres Straits (Australia) via Africa and even parts of Europe, such as the Highlands of Scotland and high alpine Switzerland, and the book he eventually produced was *Nutrition and Physical Degeneration.*

One thing you have to realise here is that dentition isn't just about your mouth and face. Dental development and health are a strong, as well as immediately visible, index of overall health and fitness. It's not for nothing that we place so much store by a beautiful, properly developed, symmetrical face. People whose faces are in decay are in decay more broadly. If you have a narrow face with crowded, rotting teeth and thin nostrils, you will, as a whole person, invariably be unhealthy.

Price discovered at least a dozen – I think it was 14 – traditional groups who were in "perfect physical condition" as a result of continuing their traditional diet. People like the Maasai, the Torres Strait Islands, Crofters in the Scottish Highlands, the Inuit. The traditional diets of these people varied from place to place, of course, but they were all built on the same foundation of nutrient-dense animal foods, especially organs like liver, fatty cuts of meat, eggs and seafood. Wherever traditional groups had given up these foods for modern industrial food, the same physical problems Price saw in his practice in Ohio were visible.

One of the most useful things Price did to support his thesis was take lots of pictures, and the most striking ones are direct comparisons of identical twins, one of whom still ate the traditional diet and the other, who had given it up. One looks great, the other not so much. With these direct comparisons it's basically impossible to argue with Price's thesis, and I'm not alone in thinking that he actually formulated ironclad scientific rules for human health and development. These form the backbone of my case for a return to ancestral nutrition.

I think I ought to say, since we're talking about vegetarians and vegans, that they get one thing right at least: that industrial

Clockwise from above: Regenerative farmer Joel Salatin; Russian philosopher Alexander Dugin; WEF founder Klaus Schwab

GRECO GUM
gum from Chios, Greece
nbr. 1.59 oz (45 g)
A WORKOUT FOR YOUR FACE, IN YOUR POCKET.

agriculture, especially the raising of livestock, is an abomination. It is. But what they get wrong is their insistence that this is the only way to farm animals, with the implication that livestock cannot and should not be raised full stop. No, we don't have to raise animals in concentration camps. Torture need not be involved. There are other ways. In fact, until very recently we raised animals in an entirely different manner, and that's what proponents of regenerative agriculture, which is very important to *The Eggs Benedict Option*, advocate returning to.

You draw heavily on Alexander Dugin's work, specifically, the *Great Awakening vs the Great Reset*. Your book, I would say, offers a concrete, practical solution for the Great Awakening. How has Dugin influenced you in writing the EBO?

Dugin is a very interesting character who's been in the news recently for unhappy reasons [his daughter was assassinated a few weeks ago in a car bomb that was clearly intended for him]. I've only read a small amount of his work, including some of *The Fourth Political Theory*, but what he says in his short book on the Great Reset is very interesting and useful for my purposes in *The Eggs Benedict Option*.

First of all, he offers us a compelling "genealogy" of the Great Reset, showing that it has a deep history and metaphysics that can be traced back to the Middle Ages and the emergence of a new philosophy known as nominalism. For the nominalists, basically, there were no such things as universal entities, only individual entities, in opposition to what the Platonists and Aristotelians (referred to as "realists" or "universalists") believed. Now, the relevance of this might not be immediately obvious to you, but what the victory of nominalism entails, ultimately, is the dis-

solution of all forms of collective identity. Nominalism has been an acid-bath for tradition in the West, beginning with the Reformation; continuing through the emergence of capitalism and liberalism, and the triumph over fascism and communism in the twentieth century ("the End of History"); and culminating in the Great Reset. All forms of collective identity, whether we mean religion, race or ethnicity, gender and now even what it means to be a human being ("posthumanism") have been or are being undermined by the nominalism that is at the heart of modern Western thinking. This is the kind of deep history of the Great Reset that we need, rather than speculation about ancient bloodlines etc. It allows us to see that the Great Reset is, in a very real sense, merely an outgrowth of this trend – the dominant trend? – in Western intellectual, social and political life, including the emergence of liberalism. Fully understanding this means, among other things, that we can't solve the problem of the Great Reset with more liberalism (the liberal's favourite solution). We need to think differently if we want to get out of this trap.

As well as this genealogy, Dugin also offers an interesting account of what he calls "The Great Awakening". This is the global resistance that has emerged to globalism and the Great Reset, whether we mean Trump and QAnon, Putin's Russia, Islamic regimes like Iran, or the CCP. At present, most of this resistance is spontaneous and largely untheorised, but Dugin sees the potential for a more coordinated front against globalism, in which different nations or civilisations draw on their own native resources to resist the globalist vision of the future. Although I'm not entirely sure how much common ground nations like the US and China, or the US and Iran, can find, I do think that the idea of looking within – looking to alternative traditions in our history – and also looking to other, non-Western traditions, is one powerful way that we can imagine a new future.

Russia also inspired you in the latter part of the book when looking at agricultural practices. You recommend we look at their 'dachas' as a model of household agriculture that we should consider implementing in the West.

This is precisely what I mean by looking to alternative traditions both within and outside our own culture. Russian household gardening is an ancient practice of small-scale agriculture that goes right back to the earliest days of the first Russian kingdoms, when peasants had their own plots of land in addition to the land they tilled for the local lord. It's incredibly productive – something like 50% of all food consumed in Russia by value is produced on people's own land, 90% of the potatoes, more than 50% of the milk and 50% of the meat – and has various incredible benefits beyond the high-quality organic food it provides. Among other things, household gardening keeps people fit and healthy; provides recreation for families and friends; helps build a sense of community (most of the produce is either consumed or exchanged directly with other growers, rather than reaching the market); increases the nation's food security; reduces inflation. It also has a deep spiritual and political aspect, rooting people in the soil of Mother Russia, which has been developed in a new homesteading movement called Anastasia. I talk about this at length in the book.

Although Russia is now an industrial nation with hypersonic weapons, and the majority of people now live in the cities rather than the countryside, 35 million households spend an average of 17 hours a week during the growing season working on their gardens (which is actually about half the time the average American spends in front of the television each week). Urbanites travel out of the city to plots in the countryside, whereas those who already live in the countryside might have a garden attached to their home and some extra land somewhere else nearby. These plots of land, on average, aren't all that big, but they provide a wealth of nutrition, from fruits and vegetables to animal products, because they're farmed intensively, using all sorts of time-honoured techniques to maximise yields, like companion planting. The fact that this system has been going on for so long, and that many of the plots have been in continuous use for hundreds of years, is a testament to its sustainability.

It's ridiculous that Russian household gardening hasn't received more attention than it has, but all sorts of prejudices exist in the Western mind about Russia, not least of all the idea that it's actually a country full of alcoholics who are always millimetres away from starvation or extermination. As a result, Russian household gardening is often portrayed simply as a response to the hardship of life in Russia, rather than a deep cultural form that also has a wider potential application outside the country.

You make an interesting parallel with the US, and how this could easily be replicated there. In fact, it largely was already in practice at the turn of the century.

The US may not have an unbroken thousand-year tradition of small-scale farming, but we shouldn't forget that it began as a nation of small farmers and remained one until not all that long ago. Most of the Founding Fathers were farmers. And I think it was Thomas Jefferson who predicted that America would be in trouble if it ceased to be a nation of small farmers, echoing a very ancient Roman sentiment about the inherent virtue of the small farmer (as expressed for instance in the Horace poem, "Blessed is the man who, far from the city's business, tends his paternal herds…").

When the American frontier was finally declared closed in 1890, some, like Fredrick Jackson Turner, believed that Jefferson would be proved right. Life on the frontier, according to Turner, was what made all the disparate peoples who landed on American shores into Americans. The frontier was, in a sense, the nation's "safety valve", which allowed it to cope with the massive waves of immigration through the nineteenth century. With that gone, how would the huddled masses be assimilated and become Americans? The "Turner Thesis", as it's known, has been hugely influential, and politicians from FDR to JFK have called for the creation of new frontiers (welfare for all, science and the space race) to ensure the American nation continues to thrive.

There have also been various "back to the land" drives since the closing of the frontier, the most notable taking place during World War II, when millions of ordinary people were encouraged to grow their own food as much as possible. Various schemes have also been established, especially in impoverished urban areas, to create community gardens to provide extra food for the poor. Most of these schemes have been very successful.

I'm not sure that Russian household gardening could *easily* be replicated in the US, but I still think it could happen. Here's a fact: the total area of lawns in the US is significantly larger than the amount of land under cultivation by household gardeners in Russia. So Americans already have the space if they wanted to put it to use, without the need for things like government land grants – although these have been used to great effect before in American history (e.g. the Homestead Act). One of the main barriers, I think, is the fact that the law in America favours big farmers and corporations. The title of one of Joel Salatin's most famous essays says it all: "Everything I want to do is illegal". You would need to create a totally new environment where the little man is encouraged and empowered to produce food and exchange it in his local community, without fear of repercussion. For that, I think, you'd need a renewed populism willing to take on the big corporate interests. That's no small task, but I think it can be done.

Joel Salatin is a fascinating figure, isn't he? Can you tell us more about the kind of farming he advocates?

Joel Salatin is a really inspirational figure. One of the best ways to get into his work is either through a collection of his essays like *Everything I want To Do Is Illegal,* or to watch him on Joe Rogan. It was Rogan who first introduced me to him, a few years ago, but since then I've read a lot of his work, especially while I was writing *The Eggs Benedict Option.*

Joel has a 500 acre farm in Swoope Virginia where he's at the cutting edge of regenerative agriculture. Regenerative agriculture is a model of agriculture that goes beyond simply being sustainable. The aim is not to maintain a certain level of fecundity but actually to restore and enhance it. In this aim and in their methods, regenerative farmers like Joel Salatin are doing more or less exactly what the Russian household farmers are doing, just on a larger scale and, importantly, with the greater involvement of grazing animals, especially cows. Household farmers and regenerative farmers alike shun the use of artificial chemicals and use a variety of time-honoured techniques like cover-cropping and companion-planting, techniques which have fallen out of favour since the advent of modern fertilisers, pesticides and herbicides (the inaptly named "Green Revolution" of the mid-twentieth century).

One of the things that's most interesting about regenerative agriculture is the absolute centrality of livestock grazing to it. In the regenerative model, livestock are not only responsible for converting indigestible plant matter into the most nutritious food we can eat, but through their grazing, trampling and production of manure, they also enhance the goodness of the soil dramatically. In fact, saying that livestock are central to regenerative agriculture is actually misleading. "Essential" would be a better word, because without them the whole enterprise would fail.

This is the complete opposite of the today's industrial model of grain agriculture, which includes a significant proportion of livestock-rearing, especially in the US, since much of the grain produced is fed to livestock in concentrated animal feeding operations (CAFOs). Industrial agriculture on the standard model is often referred to as "extractive" farming, for the simple reason that it takes and takes and takes and never gives anything back. This is why, people like Salatin argue, we must go beyond mere sustainability. We've already depleted the earth's soils to such an extent that just sustaining them isn't enough: we need to restore them if we are to be able to continue farming in the long term.

The most dire predictions about the state of the earth's agricultural topsoil are that there may be as little as 60 years of agriculture left before the soils are totally exhausted. The Great Reset model of agriculture has nothing to say about how topsoil depletion will be combatted or reversed, only the confident assertion that we can feed 10 billion people an almost entirely plant-based diet simply by using new technology, including GMO and smart AI-assisted application of chemicals.

One thing people don't understand, and they should understand, is that the majority of the world's agricultural land is simply unfit for growing crops. Many people, including those who really should know better, seem to think we could just turn all the land used for grazing over to crop-growing, but they couldn't be more mistaken. Over 60% of agricultural land is what's called "marginal land", which means that it's poor quality land that's only suitable for grazing animals. Although the remaining 40% is classified as arable land, i.e. suitable for crops, the truth is that this figure is misleading. Much of the world's arable land, for instance the arable land of North Africa, is only suitable for a limited range of agricultural products, like olives. Only 3% – that's right, 3% – of all agricultural land is classed as "prime" arable land, and much of that is in central Europe and southern Russia. If we ruin that, our options are very limited.

Both of these small and large scale farming methods are what true environmentalists (a completely co-opted term for big business and the Globalists) should be advocating for, since they allow us to take from the earth whilst replenish the soils. It sounds like the ideal food ecosystem, but goes against the entire narrative of finite resources the Globalists have been propagating for decades...

Yes, but you know, there's a strange contradiction at the heart of all of this. It's not the only contradiction in what the globalists say, either. On the one hand, as you note, they bang on endlessly about finite resources, the dangers of population increase – it's all a zero-sum game and so something will have to be reduced, drastically, if we aren't to destroy the planet. And they usually say, or at least heavily imply, that this must be the world population. This is the globalism of the Club of Rome (a huge influence on the creation of the World Economic Forum) and of the Georgia Guidestones. "Maintain humanity under 500,000,000 in perpetual balance with nature", as the Guidestones had it (may they rest in piss).

On the other hand, though, with the Planetary Health Diet, you have these blithe assurances that we must continue to extract, extract, extract to produce enough food to feed a massively expanded global population. The estimate that's used in the literature for the Planetary Health Diet is 10 billion by 2050. I'm sure I'm not the only one who finds himself a little confused by this contradiction, but I think I can square the circle without having to claim that all of the writing and pronouncements I've been analysing for the book are just a smoke-screen or cover for depopulation. I think the Great Reset model, including the Planetary Health Diet, is one that the globalists will go through with if they're allowed to. In the long term, this may lead to drastic reductions in population, but I don't think that's the immediate goal.

The main theme of the Great Reset is corporate control, and the extractive model of industrial agriculture is the one that makes the most money for corporations. That's why they want to intensify, rather than abandon it. At the same time, there has to be a compelling argument to justify the dramatic transformation entailed by the Great Reset – the total surrender of individual wealth and sovereignty – and what better way to justify this than the twin threats of climate change and population explosion?

Following your discussion of these special agricultural methods, you put forward the case that they can form the basis of a 'renewed populism'. Can you elaborate on your vision?

Unlike in Russia, where the growth of homesteading movements like Anastasia has happened spontaneously, without government support, largely because small-scale agriculture is so embedded in Russian life, in America the growth of such a movement will necessarily be political. There's no other way around it – but that's not a bad thing. Far from it.

The movement that was first given the name "populism", which emerged in the late nineteenth century, was principally a movement of small-scale farmers. And they were fighting to protect their lives and livelihoods from enemies that we would recognise today: corporations and other predatory institutions like the railroads and banks. The prices of crops were declining, banks were foreclosing on family farms and the cost of using the railroads remained almost prohibitively high. Life for the ordinary hard-working man and his family was becoming unbearable. Their great leader was William Jennings Bryan, who is most famous for his "cross of gold" speech and for his later role in the Scopes monkey trial. Like Jefferson, Bryan was convinced that America would change for the worse if it allowed its small farmers to suffer. He said – and I'm paraphrasing – that you could burn down America's cities and they would spring back up again the next day, but if you burned down America's farms, the streets of every city would soon be overrun by grass.

Small-scale agriculture, then, was the original incubator of populism in the US, and I think there's just something about being a small farmer – the kind of work it involves and the kind of people who do it – that makes it necessarily so. The honest hard work; the self-reliance; the rootedness in the soil and the rhythms of the earth rather than the rhythms of money and city life. I'm sure I'm romanticising it a bit, but that doesn't make it any less true.

In my vision, populism serves a kind of dual purpose. I think there will need to be an initial popular political movement to break the corporate stranglehold on agriculture and US politics. Of course this will find support in rural communities, but those communities are not the same as the communities of the 19th century. There are nowhere near as many farmers as there once were. Urban communities will be more important, but they have much to gain, not least of all access to better quality food. If the corporate system is broken up, and the government provides incentives to small farmers, perhaps to adopt regenerative methods, then we will see, potentially, another kind of populism emerge that flourishes once again among a multitude of small farmers.

But breaking up the corporate system, which has already caused so much damage to the health of the nation and to the environment, and which has warped the government's political priorities both at home and abroad, will have to be the main priority.

The book is a warning: the Globalists have a near total control over our food supply chain, and they are aiming for full control by the year 2030, in accordance with their stated plans (the Great Reset and the UN's SDGs). The next moves to accelerate their consolidation are already in motion: artificial food scarcity/famine as a result of the manufactured Ukraine crisis, farmers going out of business due to governments' 'ecological' policies and acquisition of land, to name a few. Tell us about the future that awaits in terms of

the type of food we would consume and the allowance system along with it, should they succeed.

So, as I've said, the Planetary Health Diet – the new global diet developed by the EAT Foundation, a partner of the WEF – is almost entirely plant-based. Even though it allows for some consumption of traditional animal products, the amounts are token amounts, which is why it's best to see the diet as a plant-based diet rather than an omnivorous one. The amounts of traditional animal products are so small – a quarter of a large egg and maybe a wafer-thin slice of meat a day – because their carbon footprints, as we're endlessly told, are just so bad.

Given that climate change, together with global population growth, is the principal justification for the need to transition to the Planetary Health Diet, it's likely that adherence to the diet would be ensured through a personal carbon allowance. Basically, everyone has a personal allowance of emissions they can "spend" on services and commodities, including the food they eat. It's possible that these allowances will be earned through working, but I think it's more likely that they'll simply be administered as a form of universal basic income. AI and automation – the much-vaunted Fourth Industrial Revolution – are going to make the majority of workers totally redundant, so there isn't going to be any work for them to do – unless our globalist overlords decide to get us all walking on giant treadmills for eight hours a day, like the inmates of a nineteenth century British prison. I think the scheme will be tied to a Chinese-style social credit score too – just look at what happened to the truckers in Canada who had their banking frozen – so it may be the case that bad behaviour will result in reductions in your allowance.

It's very important to realise that you don't need to make meat illegal to prevent people from eating it. You just have to make it so expensive – either in monetary terms, as we're seeing now, or in terms of its carbon cost – that it's beyond the reach of ordinary people. If the decision is "Do I have a Beyond Meat burger and heat my home or do I have a real burger and not heat my home?" most people are going to choose the plant-based alternative and warmth. People are making such decisions right now, as the economic downturn starts to bite. It's already in the headlines that meat consumption is massively down due to inflation, and things are only likely to get worse this winter.

As far as the actual practicalities of using the system are concerned, we're obviously talking about a credit card or banking app. As long ago as 2007, the Labour government in Britain commissioned a detailed study into individual carbon allowances, on the assumption that such a system would use a credit card of some sort.

But that was fifteen years ago, and we're well past hypotheticals now. Now we have credit cards that allow you to track your carbon footprint in real time, and restrict your spending on that basis, rather than your financial means. There's the DO Black card in Sweden, a partnership between a fintech startup and Mastercard, which allows you to see the emissions generated by every purchase you make using the card. The card has a set emission limit, so you can't pollute too much, and offers various options to offset your emissions as you spend. So the technology is ready; although its use is voluntary at present. All that's needed is the infrastructure to support it on a global scale, and the political will to make people use it, whether they want to or not.

The EBO ends on an encouraging note.

We will defeat the Globalists, and we won't eat the bugs! Please share some of your optimism to close, as many will undoubtedly benefit from it in these trying times.

Absolutely. We can win – we will win! I have no doubt about this. As terrifying as the threat of a total globalist victory is, nothing about it is certain. Yes, these people are extremely powerful and, yes, they've got us on the back foot, but it will take far less to defeat them than you might think.

As the famous meme says, "If the situation were truly hopeless, their propaganda would be unnecessary." Not just the propaganda though: all of the absolutely desperate things the regime has been doing, especially in the US, to accelerate collapse and rig the political system. They're a sign of weakness as much as strength. Just look at the presidency of Donald Trump, for all its faults and failures. I believe it should be a cause for hope. The relentless attacks, the all-or-nothing attempts to smear, discredit, silence and nullify him – all of these things showed just how terrified the globalists are of a USA that doesn't dance to their tune. Which is why they're still doing their utmost to prevent a second Trump term. All it takes is one man and a movement, and I have no doubt that the behaviour of the regime will radicalise more and more people and make them realise what is truly at stake.

This isn't reason to be complacent. In fact, we must be much more vigilant and much more active than we have been thus far. I don't think we can just "trust the plan" as the QAnon people would have us do. We all need to be working hard, building friendships, building local networks and spreading the word. Because we have everything to gain – but also everything to lose if we fail.

Wait! Last but not least, we must talk about the upcoming Tucker Carlson Originals documentary on masculinity, coming out this fall. Judging by how people completely lost their minds when the trailer came out, it's fair to say we can expect a total meltdown of the Internet when the whole thing drops! Having had an early viewing thanks to you, I can say it is just SO GOOD.

If the entirety of the last two years still feel like something of a dream, this Tucker documentary is definitely the part I'm having the hardest time believing. I watched the documentary for the first time with one of my best friends and, honestly, we stood in stunned disbelief for the entire 35-or-so minutes, then immediately watched it again from the start to make sure we hadn't just imagined it. But it really is real! Obviously I have to keep the details close to my chest, but let's just say that it's going to enrage all the right people, delight all the right people and help spread our message to a far wider audience than ever before. I can't think of a bigger white-pill at this moment in time. ETA is October. Get ready! 

The Eggs Benedict Option *is available now directly from antelopehillpublishing.com, or from Amazon, Barnes and Noble, Book Depository and other third-party retailers.*

Visit noorbinladin.com for links to all of Noor's writing and to her podcast, Noor Bin Ladin Calls, including two interviews with Raw Egg Nationalist.

AS BAD AS THEY COME

fiction **BY DETECTIVE WOLFMAN**

Los Angeles, California. 1953. There's something bad brewing in Hollywood, and only the baddest of bad men is up to the task.. Thrilling archeypal fiction from DETECTIVE WOLFMAN.

Dutch Van Zandt read the ransom note.

$50,000 or the dame gets it was the gist. The dame was Dorothy Malone, a B-movie beauty with a classy rep and no studio attachments. She was a worker, not a star. Not the kind of woman you try to ransom if you know what you're doing. But star or not, she was hip deep in some Western at R.K.O. and the suits were apoplectic.

The kidnappers identified themselves as the *Band of the Left Hand.* Sounded like limp-dick commies with the blacklist blues. Contact had been made and forty-eight hours given to come up with the dough and wait for further instructions.

Amateur hour. Not that it bothered Dutch. Kidnap jobs were always a gas, and a kidnapped actress meant all bets were off.

Security Consultant. It was a fancy term for a fixer and a goon, but it suited Dutch just fine. He made a slick living bird-dogging and bull-dogging for studio brass. Fast cash from fat cats.

It was a job for a bad man, and Dutch was as bad as they come.

Life was grand.

He was parked on the street in his Roadmaster with the top down. Dorothy Malone had a nice little one-story in Brentwood. Flowers in a little garden out front. No car in the driveway. He put the note in the glove box and let himself in through the back.

The door opened into the kitchen. It was tidy with a coffee cup and saucer in the sink. The chairs were pushed in neatly under the little table and the framed photos of ma and pa back in Texas were perfectly situated.

He saw the bowls on the floor just as he heard the deep growl behind him. He turned and saw a big, beautiful, but none-too-pleased German Shepherd showing teeth.

Dutch played it low and cool. At six-foot-six and two-forty he could break the dog's neck if he needed to but he hoped that he didn't. The big, bad man was a soft touch when it came to animals. A holdover from his Montana boyhood. Not even the War could take that from him.

"Easy, big fella," he said in a soft voice, slowly crouching down. The dog took a step back and gave a nasty bark. He flicked his fangs with his tongue the way dogs do when they're two seconds from tearing out your throat.

"Don't look at me like that." Dutch

slowly reached over to the ice box and pulled it open. Sure enough he found a fat prime rib waiting there like it was meant to be.

Thank God for Texas gals.

"I bet you're hungry, aren't you." He pulled out the steak and watched the dog's fury wither into wet-eyed longing. He held out the meat.

"Come on, buddy, I won't hurt you."

The dog came forward but stopped short, unsure. He gave another bark that was undercut with a whine. His paws padded nervously back and forth.

"Come on."

Finally the dog relented. Dutch's massive hands moved across his fur with a tenderness that didn't suit them. The dog wolfed down the steak and lapped at Dutch's face to show his gratitude and remorse.

"No hard feelings," Dutch rubbed behind the dog's ears. "Where's your mama, huh? Where did she go?"

He filled the water bowl and opened the back door. While the dog drank his fill and ran around the yard Dutch walked the rest of the house. It was more of the same. Modest but meticulous decorations and lived-in cleanliness. Photos of family and friends in place of expensive art. A crucifix on the wall in the living room.

He recalled the bookstore scene in *The Big Sleep*. Bogie comes in out of the rain and there's our girl. Brunette, bespectacled, and sharp as a fresh razor. She drops the glasses. Lets the hair down. And closes up shop to drink private-eye rye and wait out the rain with the Man, himself.

Dutch torched for her even then. He always did have a soft spot for dark-haired Irish girls.

He did a sweep of the medicine cabinet and the bedroom but found nothing out of the ordinary.

No signs of a struggle. Whoever took Dorothy Malone didn't do it here.

The cozy house yielded no clues but it gave Dutch a feeling for who the missing woman was. Head a little in the clouds but feet firmly on the ground. A little whimsy and a lot of heart.

The dog found him again in the living room and licked his hand. Dutch topped off his food and water before he left.

He parked in front of the Del Monte and had to crouch to get through the door. His massive frame spooked a woman coming out. He gave her his best grin and held the door. The woman was all batting eyelashes and passed by so close it almost got biblical.

His grin took a sinister edge as he set eyes on Fred Shine at the far end of the bar. Shine was a muckraker for the *Herald* and knew more of L.A.'s dirty secrets than the Devil himself. Shine smiled. He looked like a possum in a bow tie.

"Hiya, Van Zandt," the possum said. "Buy me a drink?"

"Bum me a smoke?"

"Of course. What are friends for?"

"Who's a friend?"

Shine went theatrical, with a hand over his heart.

"You wound me, big guy."

"Don't worry. Something tells me you'll make it."

"Damn straight. I'll never die."

"What are you drinking?"

"Sazerac."

"Coonass."

"Thug."

It went on like that for a while. The low-blow back and forth of pals-by-necessity. Loathsome to the common man, the wolf and the rodent share a small kinship. Thus was the lot for men who made their living in the wake and filth of the rich and powerful.

But what a living.

"Give me the goods on the *Band of the Left Hand*," Dutch said after a hearty swig of beer. Shine took clipped drags off a Chesterfield and blew the smoke through his nostrils.

"I got nothing concrete. I just hear rumors."

"I like rumors," Dutch said.

"Well I hear the Band is bad news, baby. Steer clear."

Dutch raised an eyebrow.

"I ain't scared of Hollywood reds, Fred."

"Oh they're red, all right," Shine said. "But not the way you mean." Shine took a drink for dramatic effect, the bent little prick. "They're devil worshipers." Shine wiggled his eyebrows.

"No shit?" Dutch said.

"And the little birds tell me they've killed people. Actual human sacrifice."

"Jesus."

"Amen."

"Where do I find them?"

"Beats the hell out of me," Shine said with a shrug. Dutch had to admit, the thought of beating the hell out of Fred Shine had no small share of appeal. But the little man's utility, and the wicked glee he derived from it amused Dutch too much.

He just stared at Shine, waiting him out. It took less than a minute.

"But I heard a rumor."

"Take your time," Dutch said. And the son of a bitch did. He took a sip of his saze-rac and a lingering drag of the Chesterfield. Dutch was still as a statue. He didn't tap his feet. He didn't fidget. He didn't even blink. It was an affect that unnerved people and

Shine was no exception.

"There's a fella by the name of Herb Becher. He runs the Vanguard Playhouse on Franklin. Ever been?"

"Can't say that I have."

"You leg-breakers are all the same. You got no culture."

"Culture. That's another word for fungus, ain't it?"

"You're a riot," Shine said. "Anyway, I hear whispers that Becher is a major player in subversive circles."

"Guys like that are a dime a dozen, Fred." Dutch countered.

"Becher got popped last year for fooling around with underage girls. When they raided his place they found all kinds of weirdo junk."

"Weird how?"

"Weird like witchcraft, sex magick – real occult shit."

"Guy sounds like a pervert."

"Pervert, pinko, probably half a swish. But he lawyered up good and beat the kiddie rap. If I were you I'd start with Becher."

Dutch finished his drink, slipped Shine a c-note and walked back out into the light.

Franklin Boulevard was paradise for stakeouts. It was all little shops and restaurants, teeming with pretty pedestrians and loquacious loafers. Dutch lounged like a jungle cat in the Roadmaster.

Sleeves up.

Top down.

His big left arm bent at the elbow, propped on the car door and holding a white paper cup of hot coffee. His big right arm stretched out across the seat with a cigarette between his fingers. He was parked

His grin took a sinister edge as he set eyes on Fred Shine at the far end of the bar. Shine was a muckraker for the Herald and knew more of L.A.'s dirty secrets

across the street and half a block down from the Vanguard Theater. On the seat next to him was an 8x10 of Herb Becher.

Beach bum tan with an ascot and a smile like a pauper's graveyard. Not exactly Alan Ladd.

Dutch's cool gaze went from the photo to the canary yellow Bel Air parked in front of the theater. The car was registered to Becher but Dutch could have sussed that out with a glance. The marquee said they were putting on some show called *Woyzech* in a couple weeks. He couldn't tell if that was Kraut or Polack.

The coffee cup got lighter and the cigarette got shorter. No one came in or out of the theater. The bright blue sky turned tangerine. It was like that sometimes. Hurry up and wait.

Dutch bought some hotdogs from a fat man with a cart. Sure enough, when he was halfway through his third dog Herb Becher sashayed out of the theater in a silk shirt and too-high slacks. He had a sloppy little gang of ugly hangers on nipping at his heels. They all piled into Becher's Bel Air.

Dutch legged it back over to his ride and fired up the engine as Becher was pulling into traffic. He wolfed down the dog and hit the gas.

Becher hooked the Bel Air around and headed east. Dutch followed him nonchalant all the way to Los Feliz. Spit-shined sidewalks and immaculate lawns gave way to starter homes with chipped paint and weeds drooping like stumble-bums over the sidewalk. The Bel Air slowed and pulled into a driveway. The house was the same canary yellow, if faded. Dutch cruised on

by, turned up the nearest cross street, and parked under the looming canopy of a magnolia tree. It was nearing full dark and the buds were closing up shop for the night.

He walked back to Becher's place and peeked in the windows. The curtains were drawn but they were thin and sheer. His nighttime eyes saw plenty.

Becher and those other geeks in the living room. One of them was slinging Satanic sermons with socialist overtones while another one set up a film projector. Becher left the room. Dutch walked around the side of the house, peeping windows.

Office. A mess of books packed into shelves that had never been dusted.

Bathroom. Toilet seat up and grunge on the shower curtain.

Bedroom. A naked woman tied to a dirty bed. A mattress soaked with blood.

Go cold. That's what most people do when they see the signature of violence writ large. But not Dutch. He felt a warm little fire spark in his chest and course through his veins like liquid heat. A thrill and a comfort all at once – like that feeling he got as a kid from the smell of pine sap and cinnamon on Christmas morning – that's the feeling that came over Dutch. The powerful muscles in his broad shoulders relaxed. Only his monstrous fists were clenched.

He walked around to the back of the house and found Becher standing over a brick fire pit. He threw in a mess of bloody sheets, sprayed them with lighter fluid, and lit them up.

Dutch stalked out into the night. As he drew closer to the fire and to his prey all thoughts of yesterday and tomorrow dissi-

Go cold. That's what most people do when they see the signature of violence writ large. But not Dutch. He felt a warm little fire spark in his chest and course through his veins like liquid heat

pated like cigarette smoke.

He was thoroughly entrenched in the electric NOW.

Breath to breath.

Heartbeat to heartbeat.

The palm of his right hand covered Becher's mouth and nose with a perfect seal. The little man's stifled cry tickled his hand and gave him a brief memory of catching fireflies. Dutch grabbed Becher's arm with his left hand.

"Don't struggle," he cooed in Becher's ear. "You're mine. You struggle or scream and I'll break you in half. Do you understand?"

Becher nodded as best he could. Dutch held him like a vice.

"I'm gonna ask you some questions, Herb. And I want you to answer just as calm and quietly as I ask them. If you fuck with me or I think you're lying I'll hold your face in that fire until your eyes melt."

Becher whimpered.

"Don't cry," Dutch warned. "It makes me mad." He looked into the fire and saw the sheets cooking.

"Is that Dorothy Malone's blood?" He relaxed his palm just a tad. Becher shook his head.

"No," he whispered.

"Whose blood is it?"

"No one's."

Dutch pulled Becher's arm up behind his back and heard the man's shoulder dislocate. He screamed into Dutch's palm.

"You've got a lot of joints, Herb, and I've got all night. Think before you speak. Whose blood is it?" He lifted his palm. It was wet with tears and snot.

"Just a girl," Becher whispered frantically. "I don't...I think her name was Joanne or Josie, something like that."

"She the girl tied to bed back there?"

"Yes." He was blubbering now.

"I know you're with the *Band of the Left Hand*, Herb. I know you've got Dorothy Malone stashed somewhere. She alive?"

"Yes!" he moaned.

"Where is she?"

"1206 Kings Way! Just south of Laurel Canyon."

"Who else is there?"

"Lots of us. And the Magus."

"The Magus?"

"He's in charge."

These people, Dutch thought. "So this was all his bright idea?"

"NO!" Becher whisper-whimpered. "The dead girl. She and some of the others acted on their own. They named the *Band*. The Magus made examples of them."

"And he threw you a bone, huh?" Dutch felt Becher try to straighten up and grasp for some last minute dignity.

"The Magus rewards the faithful," Becher said. "He is powerful. He'll make you beg for mer-"

Dutch broke Becher's neck. It always surprised him how easy it was. He pushed the dead man over into the fire pit.

He pulled his .38. It looked like a toy in his massive mitt but it would do the job.

He went in through the back door and followed the sound of the sermon. He stepped into the living room and caught the scene quick. The preacher was four-eyed and bow-tied but otherwise passed for normal. His congregation was another matter. A fella built like a scarecrow with a haircut straight out of the Middle Ages sat on a ratty sofa next to a bookish broad with a uni-brow. A third dunce sat on the floor looking up at the talker like a fat Harpo Marx.

The projector was running a porno in tandem with the sermon. A free-for-all of flesh. Guys and girls writhing in a sea of skin, prostrating and supplicating to a tall man who wore the head of a black goat like a mask.

The malignant moviegoers looked at Dutch all glassy-eyed and confused. There was a moment of silence like you get just before lightning strikes. Dutch popped the three ghouls with the .38. Two head-shots that were almost a hat-trick but the fat boy tried to get up and the bullet caught him in the throat. He made this wheezing sound while he drowned on the dirty rug.

The preacher eyeballed Dutch. He was somewhere in that soupy void between shock and terror.

"You really worship the Devil?" Dutch asked.

"Yes," the preacher blubbered.

For some reason Dutch thought that was the funniest damn thing. But the joke went sour when he saw the girls in the skin flick making meat of themselves for the ravenous ram.

That sick bastard had Dorothy Malone.

Dutch shot the little red preacher twice in the face. On his way out the door he took out his lighter and lit the curtains on fire.

The front room was fully ablaze when he drove past in the Roadmaster. He could already hear sirens in the distance. With the top down and the wind up he caught a whiff of Becher cooking in the fire pit and the smell made him miss the War.

1 206 Kings Way was a fortress. One of the Frank Lloyd Wright jobs peppered throughout the hills, it loomed like an Aztec monument carved into the mountain path. Dutch reloaded his .38, grabbed a 12-gauge out of the trunk, and hoofed it up the dark and quiet street toward the mansion. He hugged the treeline all the way to the gate and followed the wall of hand-carved stone to the lowest point in the terrain. He set the shotgun against the wall and pulled himself up. From there he clocked the cars in the massive horseshoe driveway.

It was a full house. He hopped back down, grabbed the shotgun, and kept moving to the far corner of the wall.

He went over. His instincts took control. As his body moved – climbing, rolling, ducking – his mind went back to '43.

Romania.

His squad had to seize a German communications hub inside an old castle in the village of Bran. It was all in the name of safeguarding an air raid on German fuel reserves. Operation Tidal Wave. All that time in the thick of it, Dutch had never been scared. He wasn't afraid of any man on earth, or even of dying. But in that village, in that castle, Dutch could feel something in the air, the soil, the stones of the castle walls. It was something old that reached all the way back to the deepest primordial pool.

Something evil.

Something *wrong*.

Dutch was one of twelve men that went into that castle and one of three that came back out. That was the only time he'd ever felt that old and evil feeling – until now.

The house had three floors. Dorothy would be on the third. The highest point.

He climbed to the second level. Most people didn't lock their doors or windows on the second level, maybe devil worshipers didn't either. He found a plate glass window that was ready and willing. He let himself in. He made his way through the twisting corridors, past the expensive art and Old World trophies on the walls. There were animal pelts, horns, and heads – spears and axes made of wood and stone and iron.

And the HEAT. The mansion was sweltering.

Dutch could hear commotion coming from the first floor. He could feel the density of the crowd beneath him. He saw stairs leading to the third floor but caught the glimmer of warm light from below. As he made it to the end of the hallway he peeked past the corner and down into the sprawling living room and saw the source of the deep hum throughout the house.

Chanting. Or rather, a hymn in some language that wasn't English. Two lines of sycophantic supplicants on either side of the living room, wearing dark, hooded robes and chanting dark verses.

In the middle of the floor was a man and a woman rutting in sweaty savagery. And seated in a large chair in front of a roaring fire in the ornate hearth was the Magus; tall and lean, and naked but for the black goat head he wore over his own. The light of the fire and the shadows of the moving bodies must have been playing tricks on Dutch's eyes because the Magus's limbs looked abnormally long.

The voices grew louder in tandem as the couple on the floor approached their ecstatic finish. And as they reached climax the devoted onlookers all drew knives and fell on them in a stabbing storm.

Dutch dashed up the stairs while they were distracted. He moved with exceptional speed and silence for a man his size. He opened each door in the hallway, searching for the woman.

Nothing.

Nothing.

Jackpot.

She was in a small bedroom, taped to a chair in nothing but her slip with a black cloth bag over her head. He walked over to her and put his hand where her mouth would be, but much more gently than he had with Becher.

"I'm not going to hurt you." he whispered. "I'm here to get you out. Do what I say and you'll be just fine."

She nodded. Dutch took the bag off her head. The bastards had gagged her. He pulled a switchblade from his jacket and cut the tape that held her arms. She pulled the gag from her mouth.

"Are you a cop?" she asked.

"I used to be."

"If you kill these twerps it can be our little secret."

Dutch thought that was funny. She got up from the chair but her legs wobbled and she fell to the ground.

"Damn pins and needles," she said.

"Here," Dutch said. He grabbed one of her stunned legs and began rubbing feeling back into it. It was a nice leg. She rubbed the other. Dutch looked into her eyes. She seemed steady enough. He figured she hadn't seen anything like the horror show downstairs. He was relieved at the thought.

His hands worked up to her knee and she gave them a little smack.

"Watch it, buster." She said. Dutch grinned.

"How did they ever take you alive?"

The bedroom door opened and a skinny little shit with a bandage on his ear stepped into the room. Dutch was on him in a flash and gave him the neck treatment, but this time it was messy. The guy's head did a full one-eighty and the skin split open from his ear to his Adam's apple. Blood sprayed the walls. Dutch lowered him to the floor and went back to Dorothy.

She had some feeling in her legs now, all right.

Dutch opened the window. The top of the second floor formed a rampart right outside. He turned to Dorothy.

"You're getting out of here. It's easy enough to climb down if you follow the edge of the house. It will take you all the way to the street." He handed her his car keys. "My Buick is at the end of the road. Take it and get out of here."

"What about you?" she asked.

"I'll find my way."

He helped her out the window. She

turned around. Her head just above the sill. She was one hell of a vision in the moonlight.

"Wait," she said. "I don't even know your name."

Dutch smirked. He leaned his face out the window.

"It's Dwight," he said. "But everybody calls me Dutch."

Dorothy stood up on her tiptoes, kissed his cheek, and hit him with a look that would have made a lesser man swoon.

"Go get 'em, Dutch." She turned and made her way across the crenelated rooftop. He should have followed her out and been done with it but he knew that he couldn't. Couldn't let this lie. He knew he was a bad man – as bad as they come. But he wasn't like the Magus or his cronies.

He wasn't evil.

And even though he was sure that when he died he'd go to the same Hell as they would, that didn't mean they got to live in the same world as he did.

Dutch grabbed the 12-gauge and opened the door.

When he stepped out of the room they were waiting for him at the end of the hallway.

They screamed in unison and rushed him. He couldn't tell how many. Just a black mass of gaping maws and sharp knives in the dark. He fired into them.

BAM! One of them took it right in the chest and flew back into the mob.

BAM! Another one lurched forward and caught it in the head. Their skull exploded into the eyes of the one behind them.

BAM! Two for one. But they kept coming.

BAM! A woman shrieked as half her face came off. She ate the floor as the others trampled her.

BAM! The last one spun like a top and Dutch lifted the shotgun just as the next man brought down his blade with an overhand stab. Dutch deflected it and hit them so hard with the butt of the 12-guage that he pinned his head to the wall and felt his skull crack like a hard-boiled egg. He kicked the next apostle so hard in the midsection they let out a wheezing sound like a wounded mule. As they pitched forward he swung the shotgun like a club into the top of their head and shut them up forever.

But the work was not done. Still more came for him. He took a slash to the shoulder as he stiff-armed one of them. He pulled his revolver with the other hand and shot the knifeman point blank in the face. They drove him back. Ferocious as he was they were not afraid of him. They were a far cry from Becher and his lackeys. He would have to kill them all.

Dutch smiled.

He spent his last five shots in two more screamers but got stabbed in his gun-hand. He dropped the .38 and crouched down just in time to dig his shoulder into the middle of a charging congregant and throw him over his back. The assailant rolled onto his stomach to push himself up but Dutch pinned him to the floor with a foot in the base of his back. With his foot planted, Dutch reached down, grabbed the man's face with both hands, and yanked upward. There was a crack like thunder.

Dutch stood up straight, taking deep breaths of the hot, blood-charged air. His powerful muscles dripped sweat and blood. The dead man at his feet was the last of the black-robed fanatics.

Deep laughter came from the far end of the hall.

Deeper than the grave.

Deeper than Hell.

The Magus stood at the edge of the stairs, laughing at his dead followers. Laughing at Dutch. He was a towering black shape in the darkness, wreathed by the flickering light of the fire below.

"Come and get it," Dutch said.

The Magus stopped laughing and said something foreign that Dutch couldn't make out. The strange, vile man let out a low growl and charged forward.

With so many bodies in the way Dutch was counting on him to lose his footing and pitch forward with the weight of the goat head but thc crafty bastard never missed a step. He just came on faster and faster. As he closed the distance Dutch could see just how big and formidable the madman was. He was poised to ram Dutch with the goat horns, and with so little room to maneuver Dutch had to think fast. He picked up one of the discarded knives off the floor and threw it straight ahead. He didn't dare to hope that it would stick but the Magus moved his head just enough that when they collided Dutch only took a glancing blow from the horns.

They went down. They hit the floor so damn hard they could barely hold onto each other. There was no time for guile and no room for finesse. They choked and shoved and stiff-armed as they scrambled to get to their feet. The Magus was all long, ropy muscle – strong and quick.

They traded blows, crashing into the hallway walls, shattering decorations and scattering drywall as they pummeled each other.

Dutch dealt damage that would have devastated another man. But the monstrous Magus gave as good as he got.

Dutch slugged him the short ribs but he reached out, fast as a snake, grabbed Dutch's face and smashed his head into the wall. Dutch stumbled and swung a right hook that missed the mark. The Magus smacked him in the jaw with a back fist that took him off his feet. Dutch crashed into the bodies on the floor. The Magus stalked

toward him. Dutch's head swam. The freak must have really rang his bell because he could have sworn he saw the goat eyes blink.

He knew he was in trouble. He reached under the mess of bodies, searching desperately with his hands. The Magus loomed over him. He grabbed Dutch by the hair and lifted him with one hand, and reared back to strike with the other. Just before he could bring down his fist and put Dutch's lights out for good, Dutch's hand found a knife and he shoved the blade with all his strength in between the Magus's legs.

The scream was a howl from Hell.

Dutch had never heard a sound so awful in all his life. He stumbled to his feet and crashed into the wall, knocking one of the trophy weapons loose. It was a primitive ax from the old, bad world. Dutch hefted it up and while the Magus lurched over, yowling and clutching at his gushing wound.

Dutch swung the old weapon hard and true and took off the wailing goat head in one clean swipe. A geyser of thick blood poured forth. It looked black in the dim light.

The goat head lay among the dark robes of the dead. Its lifeless black eyes gazed up at Dutch. He gazed back and wondered what Hell was like for devil worshipers.

Dorothy Malone was parked in front of the gate with the motor running.

"Need a lift?"

Dutch walked to the driver's side.

"Allow me," he said. Dorothy slid over the smooth bench seat.

"You're hurt," she said.

And he was.

"I've been hurt worse," he said.

And he had.

He got in and took them away from the wicked dead and into the living night.

It was warm enough to leave the top

down. Dutch cruised south, glancing at Dorothy. She gazed out at the hills, the wind tossing her hair. It was a damn fine head of hair. Dutch thought he wouldn't mind tossing it, himself. They drove in silence for a while, letting the breeze blow off the sheen of the nightmare palace. He made it all the way to Sunset before she spoke up.

"Where are you taking me?" she asked.

"Home."

"I don't want to go home." Dutch stopped at a traffic light. He turned and saw her staring at him.

"Where do you want to go?"

"Surprise me."

The light turned and Dutch drove ahead. Twenty minutes later they were parked at the end of a private road that stretched to the beach. Dutch had crippled a blackmailer for a swish crooner the year before so now he got to enjoy the private beach. They sat in the car, looking out at the dark tide rolling in.

"Are you cold?" Dutch asked. She shook her head.

"It's strange but I don't feel one way or another," she said. "Like I can't feel anything." Dutch took off his blazer. It was a tattered wreck but it would do. He leaned over and gently wrapped it around her.

"Better put this on just in case." The jacket nearly swallowed her up. On the screen she seemed so big and brassy but here and now she was only a little thing. He could feel her starting to shake.

"Tell me something," she said.

"What?"

"Anything. Just talk to me for a bit. Keep me from floating away." Dutch tried to think of something.

"I fed your dog," he said. "He's okay."

"Did he bite you?" she asked. "He doesn't like strange men."

"He thought about it but we're thick as thieves now. I didn't hurt him."

"I didn't think you did."

She was rubbing her arms with trembling hands.

"My God," she said. "I don't know whether to jump or lie down."

"It'll pass," Dutch told her. "Think of it like a ride at the fair and just hold on."

"What's it like to kill somebody?" She just blurted it out. No one had ever asked him that outright. And even though he'd never ruminated on it he knew just what to say to the uninitiated.

"You ever get a knot in a piece of jewelry? Like in a little gold chain?"

"Sometimes."

"You know that feeling when you work your way into the bastard and it finally comes undone?"

"Mm hm."

"It's like that. To me, anyway."

She made a quiet sound then. It was an odd sound. Not a gasp or a giggle but some kind of something.

"Could you put your arm around me, please?" she asked.

"All right."

She slid over and leaned into him hard as he wrapped his right arm around her.

"I'm not some roundheel or anything," she said.

"I didn't think you were."

"I've always gone my own way and I've never lived off anyone's good will. But they took me, you understand? And thank God for you and that things didn't go as far as they could have. I'm grateful. But I need to lean on someone for just a minute. I need to feel you here and to smell the blood and the fire on you and know that I'm alive."

He pulled her tight and rubbed some of her hair in his fingers.

He knew he was a bad man – as bad as they come. But now, more than ever in his life, he wanted to be good.

"I'm all yours," he said.

Dutch looked out at the rolling, liquid black of the Pacific. The expanse of it filled his vision and would have pulled him away but for the anchor that was the woman clinging to him in all that dark infinity. Her heart beat like an engine and her shaking body settled and warmed up in his embrace. He could feel every inch of where her body touched his own. Down to the atom.

And her smell.

Woman.

There was no dressing it up.

It was three minutes or three hours before she touched his chest, Dutch wasn't sure. He looked down at her looking up at him and when her lips met his it was fire all over again.

The night went away.

There was no yesterday.

No tomorrow.

The electric NOW between the two of them spread out and ate the whole damn world.

Detective Wolfman tweets @det_wolfman. His story Heartsfire, which appeared in an earlier issue of MAN'S WORLD, *will feature in the second* MAN'S WORLD *Annual.*

GRIT

fitness **BY GRECIAN**

Olympic weightlifting is the king of all strength sports. Blinding speed, raw power, and razor-sharp precision showcased in an biathlon of barbell events, the snatch and the clean and jerk. Thousands of repetitions and months of training distilled into six brutal lifts: three attempts to record your heaviest snatch, three attempts to record your heaviest clean and jerk. Weightlifting, as both a sporting discipline and focused mindset, rewards the bleeding edge of human adaptation. Every single day it's you versus you. Every repetition in your home gym or on the biggest competition stage is a test of your mettle. Can you quiet your mind and execute with no fear when it counts? In a nutshell, that is weightlifting.

Competitions open with the snatch, where the barbell is moved from the ground to a locked-out position overhead in one swift movement. A quarter of an inch is the dramatic difference between make and miss. Considered the more technical of the two events, the snatch demands tension, patience, and extreme accuracy from the lifter. "Barbell gymnastics" is how I describe the snatch to regular people. Move powerfully, but gracefully. Be tight, but find positions of mobility. Move as fast as you can, but don't rush through the positions. Snatching is very paradoxical, it comes and goes…sometimes you're friends and sometimes you're enemies. Even with years of experience, the snatch can elude the best of lifters when the pressure is on.

Up next is the clean and jerk, the steak and potatoes of the competition. "Snatch for the show and clean and jerk for the dough", the old heads say. Clean and jerk is a two-part movement where the barbell is pulled from the floor to the shoulders in a low front-squat position, and then jerked from the front rack to a locked-out position overhead. Raw horsepower shines here; the clean and jerk favors athletes with stocky physiques, refrigerator-thick torsos, and powerful legs. If the snatch is a finely-choreographed dance, the clean and jerk is a fistfight…in a phone booth. If you're not fully 100% mentally committed to either the clean or the jerk, you will get folded like a deck chair.

Scoring the sport is simple. Combine the top weight lifted in the snatch and top weight lifted in the clean and jerk and you have what's called a total. The lifter with the highest total and lowest bodyweight in the weight class wins. Competitions feature an array of ascending men's weight classes and an array of ascending women's weight classes, each ending with an open bodyweight division, commonly referred to as the super heavyweights.

At elite international levels, weightlifting is a sport of obscene strength and disgusting speed featuring feats of strength that shouldn't be humanly possible. Blink just once and you will miss a Chinese lifter weighing 81kg/178lbs like Lu Xiaojun snatching 170kg/374lbs like an empty bar. Tune into the super heavyweights and you'll see Georgian Lasha Talakhadze ragdoll a clean and jerk of 267kg/588lbs. However don't just take my word for it… next time you're at the gym training, load up 580lbs on a barbell. Some of us might be able to squat that, crack off a few deadlift reps, or maybe just roll it around the floor a bit. Consider for just one moment the mental fortitude it takes to pull 588lbs off the floor, then rack it on the shoulders, stand it up out of the front squat, and then finally throw it overhead – all with precision violence and controlled aggression.

Everyone loves to talk about the physical side of training the sport - the sets, the reps, the nutrition, the pharmacology, the recovery modalities. Unfortunately, far less is said about the mental side, which is arguably more important. How do athletes develop a mindset that lives outside the realm of conscious human performance? How do we design training so that the lifter dulls their senses to the danger present in constantly loading and pushing the most unnatural of movements? What conditions and variables can we control in the athlete's environment to drive the development of high-level results over multiple years?

In the West, where the sport isn't as popular, athletes often make the mistake of leaning into the physical side of the sport. "Coaching" at amateur level boils down to building up a big squat and hoping for the best, with limited technical instruction sprinkled in. It is an absolute travesty that little is done to develop the requisite mental toughness to execute in those crucial moments on the big stage. This mindset, as far as I'm concerned, is the single greatest benefit of learning the sport itself. Often the life of a weightlifter means 15 years of training the same 15 movements in gloomy gyms, an existence of comparative poverty and isolation. However there is a certain charm to the sport that draws people in, a magnetic quality that attracts masochists and produces absolute savages tapped into the immense power of the human mind and body.

Take a walk with me, I want to share a story about two men, their mindsets, and the meaning of grit in weightlifting.

True Grit - Evgeny Chigishev

The super heavyweight class is the crown jewel of Olympic weightlifting competition, where every four years one man earns the title of "the Strongest Man In The World". The super heavyweight competition in the 2008 Beijing Olympics was one for the ages, one that brings a tear to many eyes to this day. It's true that no two athletes walk the same path to the games, but those 5 rings seem to bring out the very best in us, true displays of strength and resilience. The story of Evgeny Chigishev, one of the greatest athletes you've never heard about, is one of absolute grit.

Chigishev was one of the last great Russian super heavyweight lifters of the early 2000s. Standing 6 foot 2 inches tall and weighing a muscular 131kg/290lbs, Evgeny deviated from the typical bloated, obese open-class physiognomy that produced lumbering behemoths with giant bellies. He had a striking, aesthetic physique – a wide back hewn from granite, the cannonball shoulders of a boxer, a slim torso, and hydraulic cylinders for legs. At the young age of 21, Chigishev made his Olympic debut at the 2000 games in Sydney, placing 5th overall behind monsters like Iranian Olympic Champion Hossein Rezazadeh and three-time World Champion German Ronnie Weller.

It's very difficult to explain the heady mix of pride and expectation when it comes to being a Russian weightlifter. All eyes are on you to deliver – failure to perform is not tolerated. Once you put on the national team singlet, your job is to represent the strongest people on earth by delivering results in the form of a medal, preferably gold. The 2000 games in Sydney cemented the fact that in the eyes of the Russian Weightlifting Federation, young Chigishev could very well be an Olympic champion one day. Just when Evgeny Chigishev was poised to write his name in the weightlifting history books, his life decided to take an abrupt left turn.

Shortly after Sydney, Chigishev and his training partner were lifting at the gym on New Year's Eve in December of 2001. The two lifters and good friends finished their training and left the gym in Novokuznetsk, Siberia. In one of those 'wrong place, wrong time' moments, a group of lowlifes tried to rob Chigishev and his friend at knifepoint. In the botched mugging that followed, Chigishev and his friend were both stabbed multiple times. Evgeny lost a ton of blood from a dreadful amount of stab wounds to his back and right arm, injuries that would have killed the average man. Chigishev's friend and training partner died shortly after the attack, leaving the super heavyweight lifter absolutely distraught.

Now at this stage, most people would just flat out quit, give up, call it a day. Imagine how Chigishev felt, a man who at the peak of his career had everything taken away from him in an instant. If you talk to some weightlifters, you'll find that once they lose the ability to train and compete, life begins to unwind around them. In some ways, the sport is the only thing that has given them purpose, direction, a regimen, structure, and discipline. I can't imagine the depths of despair Chigishev felt knowing that he was laid up useless in the hospital, his good friend was dead, his chance to compete at the 2004 Athens games was gone, and his future as a national team athlete was doubtful at best. But if there's one thing to learn from Chigishev, it's that there's absolutely no quit in the man, not one single ounce.

After taking a fair amount of time off, far away from weightlifting, Chigishev against all odds finds himself back in the gym. There's something familiar about the cold caress of a 20kg barbell, something that just calls you back, something restless that stirs in a weightlifter's soul. Call it resilience, call it unfinished business, call it stubbornness, call it comfort – I don't know. I can't explain these things with words here; you either feel them or you don't. By 2005, Chigishev felt them enough to be back to his previous form, silencing the critics and winning silver with solid performances at both the European Championships and the World Championships. 2007 rolls by and once again Chigishev was in excellent shape, earning a silver at both the European Championships and World Championships leading up to 2008,

How do athletes develop a mindset that lives outside the realm of conscious human performance?

the next Olympic year.

In one of the wildest weightlifting turn-arounds of all times, Chigishev entered the 2008 Olympics in Beijing as one of the class favorites, undeniably the best snatch specialist in the world at the time. He snatched a monster 210kg/463lbs, leading the competition and taking a healthy advantage into the clean and jerk. Chigishev went on to clean and jerk 250kg/551lbs to earn a silver medal, only being edged out by 1 kilo on a hail Mary third-attempt clean and jerk from German Matthias Steiner in the very last lift of the competition. Sometimes this is the nature of the sport - both pure triumph and utter heartache can be just one lift away.

In what became one of the most insane competitions ever, Chigishev left it all out on the platform but came up 1 kilo short. His journey demonstrates that sometimes true grit means losing everything, just to gain it all back.

Training couldn't take the pain away, but for Steiner the pain reminded him of his goals. As the weights on the bar increased, so too did the amount of guilt, grief and sadness he could shoulder

Execution - Matthias Steiner

The story of Austrian Matthias Steiner, the man who beat Chigishev in Beijing, is another beautiful example of grit and resilience in sport. Matthias, the son of 20-time IWF Masters (35+) World Champion Friedrich Steiner, was not a very talented lifter in his early days. His father fashioned him a small barbell and weight set but repeatedly told him to go play soccer instead. Not easily discouraged, young Matthias insisted he was going to be a weightlifter, telling his father he would be an Olympic Champion one day. Grizzly veteran Friedrich told his son that he was nuts, that it would never

happen. From that day forward, a weightlifter was born, an Olympic Champion in the making.

Competing for his home nation of Austria, Steiner had a decent junior career earning bronze medals at the 2001 European Junior Championships and 2002 European Junior Championships. Matthias kept developing and also learned how to manage his diabetes during heavy and frequent training, something that had an impact on his body weight. By 2004, Steiner competed at the Olympic Games in Athens, snatching 182.5kg/402lbs and clean and jerking 222.5kg/490lbs, which was good enough for 7th place overall representing Austria.

In 2005, the Austrian Weightlifting Federation decided to replace the national team coach, which created unnecessary tension for Steiner and others. At the European Championships that year, Steiner missed all three snatch attempts and controversy erupted over disagreements on weights selected. The coach and other federation members accused Steiner of deliberate failure and in turn, Steiner left the Austrian Weightlifting Federation and applied for German citizenship. Despite earning medals and representing his home nation in the 2004 Olympics, Steiner would not stand atop an Olympic podium in an Austrian singlet.

In the three years that passed before receiving his German citizenship, Steiner met and married a woman named Susann from Zwickau in Saxony who was impressed by his lifting on television. While their relationship blossomed beautifully, Steiner was stateless and forbidden from competing in any international weightlifting competitions for three years. Steiner found refuge training and competing for Chemnitzer AC Weightlifting Club in the independent German Weightlifting League (Bundesliga) under German national coach and mentor Frank Mantek. Under new coaching, Steiner recognized his potential as a super heavyweight lifter and committed to Mantek's training methods in the build up to the 2008 Olympics.

On July 16th 2007, Matthias Steiner received a phone call that would forever change his life. The police called him on an average summer afternoon to tell him that his wife was in a car accident and was in the hospital. By the time Matthias arrived at the hospital, the staff solemnly explained to him that they were sorry, his wife was dead, and that they had done everything that they could. Suspended in disbelief, Steiner did not know what to do with such an angry whirlwind of emotions. He stopped training for three weeks and lost nearly 20lbs in body weight, which is debilitating for any athlete preparing for the Olympics, much less a super heavyweight lifter.

Deeply depressed, Matthias received a call from Frank Mantek reminding him of his commitment to train for Beijing. Here's the point where the average person would quit, give up, tell the coach to kick rocks. But no, not Steiner. He was filled with a different kind of anger. The very next day, Mantek walked into the gym at 9am and found Matthias there, ready to train. Hurt and wounded, Steiner found a certain peace in the gym amidst the clanging and banging of barbells. Just like our friend Chigishev, the more Steiner trained, the better he felt. Training couldn't take the pain away, but for Steiner the pain reminded him of his goals. As the weights on the bar increased, so too did the amount of guilt, grief and sadness he could shoulder.

Steiner was on a religious-level tear

through competitions in 2008, this time representing Germany. Matthias won the Beijing Pre-Olympic Tournament and finished 2nd at the European Championships that year, giving him a bid to represent Germany in Beijing. At the games, Steiner found himself in a vicious three-way dogfight in the super heavyweight class with our friend and Russian favorite Evgeny Chigishev and seasoned Latvian veteran Viktors Ščerbatihs. Matthias snatched 202kg/445lbs on his second attempt, but missed 207kg/456lbs on his third, which put him in fourth place behind a very strong 210kg/463lbs snatch from Chigishev and a smooth 206kg/454lbs effort from Ščerbatihs.

Carrying the anger of his third attempt snatch miss with him, Matthias failed to clean and jerk 246kg/542lbs on his opening attempt and jaws collectively hit the floor in shock. Seeing an athlete miss an opener is never a good sign, and at this point it looked like the 2008 Olympics was over for Matthias Steiner. Chigishev then clean and jerked an easy 247kg/544lbs for a good lift on his second attempt, building even more of a lead. Just when it all seemed impossible, Coach Frank Mantek rallied Steiner to clean and jerk 248kg/546lbs on his second attempt, which at the time put him into medal contention. Answering impressively on his third attempt, Evgeny Chigishev demolished 250kg/551lbs in the clean and jerk to strengthen his lead.

At this point in the competition, there were only two men left – the Latvian Viktors Ščerbatihs and the German Matthias Steiner. Both athletes had ground to make up on Chigishev's absolutely massive 460kg total. First it was the experienced 34 year old Latvian Ščerbatihs, who attempted to increase the bar to 254kg/559lbs on his second attempt, but he missed. Feeling the pressure, Ščerbatihs jumped to 257/566lbs

Forged in Fire
MMXXII
Readers of
MAN'S WORLD
receive 20% off
USE CODE
MANSWORLD20%
AT CHECKOUT
LIMITED TIME ONLY
forgedinfireapparel.com
KNOCKOUT CLUB
Forged in Fire
Est. 2022
Forged in Fire
20 22

for his third attempt and missed that lift on the jerk, which meant his day was over. Steiner bided his time strategically and was the only man left in the competition with one lift remaining. The moments that followed continue to inspire athletes of all stripes to this day.

With a silver medal in the bag, German Coach Frank Mantek made the decision to jump 10kg/22lbs to 258kg/568lbs, which would put Matthias in the gold medal position to win the Olympics out of nowhere. This move is the sporting equivalent of gambling it all on a hail Mary touchdown attempt, a wing-and-a-prayer half-court shot, an eyes-closed walk-off home run in extra innings, winning a nail-biter penalty shootout on the last kick. In this moment, Steiner was able to free himself from the heavy chains of pain, sadness, and grief to do the impossible – he smoked his third attempt clean and jerk of 258kg/568lbs and earned himself a gold medal. One the most emotional moments of the sport followed, with Steiner first doubling over the bar screaming, pounding the platform, tears running down his face, then celebrating and jumping for joy with his coach, Frank Mantek.

Matthias Steiner stood there that day a champion, the Strongest Man in the World, with an Olympic gold medal around his neck and in his trembling hand, a picture of his late wife Susann. The man standing next to him with a silver medal around his neck – Evgeny Chigishev. Two men that had experienced tragedy and loss beyond understanding, two men that could have given up and despaired, two men that used the barbell to lift themselves up, two men exemplifying mental toughness and unwavering grit that you'll find in the sport of Olympic weightlifting. ◧

HUMAN.EXE

fiction **BY P.C.M. CHRIST**

alt"the involuntary martyrdom of the supernova" v3.194c log
datafile:546159733 class:homo sapien name:encrypted age:31 eyes:hazel height:175.26cm
(5'10) weight:69.853kg (154lb) temperature:36.1111°C (97°F) cell size:5.4m2(58sq.ft)
subject response: transcribed/encrypted
defined state: "concern" -keywords:"hello""where""somebody""help""what"
note: 1.1 defined state "concern" infers subjects pupils will dilate 1.3% normal size. di-
lation currently quantified as 1.7%. - possible defined state: "terror" 1.2 subject listed as
american male. english speaking.
1.3 eye color listed as hazel(hexadecimal #8e7618). due to lacrimation effect-redefining
eye color to aqua green(hexadecimal #80FFFE) audio log assigned: "ar"
protocol:introduction thank_you_male.mp3 run
ar:
<>hello. in an effort to maintain the sustainability of this planet. you have been randomly
selected. to give your life. as a sacrifice for others. for the greater good.</> a_humane_so-
ciety.mp3 run
ar:
   <>society is crumbling. water is scarce. food is short. children starve. earth demands res-
pite. we answer that call. as stewards of earth. stewards of society. all we do. Is only right.
only natural.</> immortality.mp3 run
ar: <>through the perception of martyrdom. your name along with countless others. will
be propelled. to a level of immortality. reverence. fame. that many humans can only dream
of.</> offspring_lie.mp3 run
ar:
   <>your offspring have been blacklisted from this glory. to ensure your genetics are car-
ried on into eternity. they are now considered an asset to humanity.</> benevolence.mp3
run
ar: <>please. take this time. to reflect on your life. before termination. as this an occasion
of grandeur. of your higher purpose. you will be given accommodations. to aid in acceptance of your fate. you see. we love you. your death is our life. we thank you.</>
biological response: lacrimation hydration -.0071%/sec. vocalizations: 210/wpm
subject response: transcribed/encrypted
defined state:"panic" -keywords:"hey""no""want""joke""why""help""wait"
note: 2.1 subject vocal range predicted to be between 87db and 110db.
ranging from 30 and 150 hertz. prediction successful.

2.2 acquired datum furthers scientific evidence that when participating in defined state
"panic" homo sapiens can be expected to achieve a vocal acuity 140-213% beyond speaking pitch.
protocol: pathos initiate searching 56151756.mem
religious association identified: protestant-christian

after_life.mp3 -volume compensation:135% run
ar:
<>jesus said to her. i am the resurrection and the life. whoever believes in me. though he
die. yet shall he live. John 11:25.</>
<>and you will be blessed. because they cannot repay you. for you will be repaid. at the
resurrection of the just. Luke 14:14.</>   <>yet a little while. and the world will see me no
more. but you will see me. because i live. you also will live. John 14:19.</>
*calculating biological evidence of psychological state in progre
ss... completed
-previous calculations suggested that due to subject's fervency toward theological sensibil-
ities subject would be spurred toward acceptance. an amount of faith should have prompt-
ed subject to find an unquantifiable amount of acceptance in own demise.
subject response: transcribed/encrypted
defined state: "denial"
keywords:"screw""god""why""real""me""dreaming""wake""somebody""help"
note:
3.1 deistic references increased 15%
3.2 protestant rejection 7.6% higher than catholic
3.3 post auditory reception. vocalizations increased 33%
3.4 experimental text versus audio reception grant approval logged protocol:logos inevita-
ble.mp3 run
ar:
<>one point seven eight people die every second. one hundred and seven every minute.
six thousand three hundred and ninety every hour. one hundred fifty three thousand
every day. the average person takes twenty eight thousand eight hundred and eighty
breaths a day. ten million five hundred forty one thousand two hundred breaths a year.
adults smile on average twenty times per day. the average reader reads seventeen books a
year. fifty one percent of the world's population believes in some sort of afterlife. there is a
one hundred percent chance that all humankind will die.</>
subject response: transcribed/encrypted
defined state: "opposed"
keywords:"don't""fuck""nobody""care""them" protocol:ethos why.mp3 run
ar:
<>you are no doubt. at this moment. angry. demanding an answer.
to the question. Why.</>
subject response: transcribed/encrypted
defined state: "threatening"
keywords:"God""kill""reason""no""fuck""never"
USER OVERRIDE login credential required username:txcooker
password:***********************

name: author_thomas_x_cooker clearance: administrative ACCEPTED
user input
-vocal manipulation set: female
-input:bf-cd-608 gooseneck desktop microphone
-output:stereo
-volume -15%
-environmental change: 50% oxygen 50% carbon monoxide
assign name: (Y/n)
Y
assigned name:Stargazer-Cons(t)olation.mp3
RECORD
0:00:00
0:01:26
<>Hi –. My name is Tommi...with an i. Listen, I know that you have questions and, unfortunately, I can't give you any answers. I don't have the authority or the capability to help you, and I am deeply sorry for that. In moments like these, I know that words seem kind of meaningless and even attempting consolation feels worthless, it just doesn't solve the problem at hand, but I would like to share something with you, and maybe it will help. I know, honey...if you could just breathe. It's okay. Inhale through your nostrils; exhale through your mouth. Good. Breathe deeper. Everything will be alright. Just breathe. Just listen to the sound of my voice. I just want to tell you a story.</> -Cell mic: muted
subject response: transcribed/encrypted
defined state: "fury"
keywords:"fuck""stupid""worthless""help""beg"
0:03:54
<>I was born and raised in the mountains of Eastern Tennessee. I was the daughter of very sad people, and poverty was a constant state of being, but they loved me and I loved them and somehow they made it work. It really is amazing,the situations that parents endure for the
good of their children, sacrifice...out of love...</>
0:04:31
<>Anyways, my parents, my grandmother and I lived on the side of a mountain surrounded by hills with even more mountains rising from behind them. It was beautiful. The trees were like...like a quilt, or waves, or something. I can't even describe it. When you saw them from on top of the mountain, it looked like the entire earth was covered in rolling green clouds with the ground nowhere in sight, with the blue of the sky, it was like I was somewhere between Earth and
Heaven. But even with that beauty in front of me everyday, I always had this thing for stars. I think the isolation brought it out; the imagination. And my imagination began with those stars. They never change, you know. Not until you really understand them. I would spend hours just looking at them. The cicadas singing harmony to the rhythm of their twinkling, and I'd just let their music take me away.</>
0:04:39
<>When I was about nine years old, we lived in a little dilapidated house, something more akin to a shack really. There were twenty-three missing shingles on the roof. It's strange how some of those little details that just come to mind when you start remembering.</>

0:06:03

<>And,classic stereotype, my mother was addicted to pharmaceutical drugs, barbiturates to be exact. She had a cousin who always brought
these bottles of thirty milligram ones.</>

0:06:44

<>And my mom...she had this big pullover dress, red with white lilies. And one of her little idiosyncrasies, I don't know why, was that every time she wore this particular dress she would cook porcupine meatballs; baked meatballs with rice mixed in with tomato sauce. And um...so one evening I see her sitting on the bed, she was drunk by then, always, and she counts her pills out, swallows them down with a plastic cup half-full of red wine, and then slides on this red dress, and then goes to the kitchen to start cooking these meatballs. Nothing new, so I'm just sitting at the table watching, sharing my attention between her and the darkness outside. And a little while later she drops a meatball, and as she bends over to pick it up she just kinda falls forward. Now you would think that I would be concerned, and I was, but I knew that when she was drunk sometimes she fell over. But then... then she doesn't get up, she starts kind of gurgling and clutching at her stomach, right, and she lets out this awful, terrifying, bloody scream. I run over and see that my mother is now bleeding from every single hole she has, and I see her face and then the white lilies on her dress are all turning this reddish brown. We found out later that she had accidentally taken a hundred milligrams of my grandmother's blood thinning medication. The insides of my mom had basically dislodged and just come pouring out, and the blood...it just kind of pooled out from underneath her. So for some reason, I just start running. It was very dark outside, the moonlight just barely making it between the trees, and I keep running, and everything is blurry and dark and red and so when I, I guess you could say "came to", I was swinging. Literally,
swinging.</>

0:08:37

<>My daddy had taken a brick and thrown a rope over a tree and hung it over a creek bed for a swing, and there I was swinging and pumping my legs harder and harder. Directly above the creek, there were no trees arched over the middle, so I would usually go there to look at the stars. And so I'm swinging looking up and the outlines of the stars are all blurry from tears that I can hear falling into puddles of water below me. Everything else was quiet, I couldn't hear nothing but tear drops falling and the quiet creak of the rope. I just keep swinging my legs as hard as I could, and every time the stars would get closer. I couldn't tell whether I was moving towards them or if they were crashing down. And every time that I went up, I wished that I wouldn't come down. Then one time, I didn't.</>

-environmental change: 40% oxygen 60% carbon monoxide
subject response: transcribed/encrypted
defined state: "disbelief"
keywords:"stars""why""believe""matter"

0:10:03

<>There was never any sensation of weightlessness or what could be described as an out-of-body experience. It was just that feeling of constant momentum when going forward on a swing, like answering the call of the void. And as I was shooting up, stars begin racing by and, for some reason, I don't even look. I just keep racing forward, numb to any pleasure or wonder from what I saw. And right as time began to dissipate from my mind, a star just

materializes directly in front of me. Just like that, and the darkness just disappears. It was, like, living inside of a kaleidoscope; silver dots with smoky pinks and blues and purples and grays. The star and I, we just gaze at one another, and then it talks to me. It says that one of the most beautiful sights that it has ever seen in all the cosmos is starlight reflecting off of tears. Of course, I start to cry, and then I learn that this star is about to go supernova. Explode. And that I would be

the first to see it.</>

0:13:41

<>It would take the inhabitants of Earth over five hundred lightyears to see its death, but I would be the sole witness of its immediate demise. It was then that every part of my sense of loss overwhelmed me; soul-crushing heart-wrecking breath-taking loss. I pleaded with the star not to die. It simply and kindly refused. I told it that it wasn't fair. Something shouldn't just die. It asked me if I had ever seen a star die. I hadn't. It said to me...it said that every star by their very design lived a life of chaos and reaction. In the deep heady cold of space all action was reaction and that all celestial bodies, even with their millennia of existence, hoped to attain acceptance of annihilation. The star said that by merely existing, though it had seen a small portion of what the galaxies had to offer, it was only through death that it might have any hope of adding to the beauty of the universe. It said that there was nothing that it could do. That it was the duty and natural process of the star to die. That by dying, it is at its most

memorable.</> 0:14:59

subject response: transcribed/encrypted

defined state: "docile"

keywords:"but""dont""want""why""children""miss""goodbye"

RECORD COMPLETE Stargazer-Cons(t)olation.mp3 archived.

Set as persuasive measure number 2 of 6

Environmental Change: 100% carbon monoxide

User Log Off

automated systems restored

note:

4.1 introduction of fictional accounts-success rate: 85.4%

4.2 instrumentation reads pulse has dropped 50% from commencement of persuasive measure.

finalexit.mp3 run ar:

  <>fare thee well traveler.</>

subject 56151756: static

moisture produced:1.274 L

-saliva:309.46mL urine:671.89mL tears:292.65mL

-bowel release mark:23.425 minutes

-deistic references:21

-expletives uttered:37 -familial references:50

conclusion: acceptance

end log sleep mode

P.C.M. Christ tweets @plzcallmechrist

INFILITRATION WON'T WORK

essay **BY JOSIAH LIPPINCOTT**

The institutions you want to infilitrate are fake and gay, says JOSIAH LIPPINCOTT. You're going to need to find another way to win.

Perhaps there is among you one of those human types who can successfully enter the belly of the monkeypox-infested bureaucratic bunkhouse — cloaking your true thoughts and beliefs for years as you slowly scramble atop the pile of HR maneaters, DMV ladies on break, and drooping manboobed administrators that make up the modern state — in order that you, at the right moment, may strike a blow for truth and justice.

Such a man is rare.

At the very least, I do not believe it can be model for the right-wing as a whole, specifically for those who lack the requisite nature for such a task. We always are who we are. We must work with what we have. The American Right is filled with those, like me, who are descendants of Scots-Irish, German, and Anglo settlers: all groups that are notoriously bad at spying, doubletalk, and lying.

It does not help that America's institutions are virtually invulnerable from internal hostile takeover. When I hear talk of trying to infilitrate institutions, parties, etc., I am deeply skeptical. The idea of making the FBI friendly to the Right or the New York Times not gay, sounds as believable as Russians successfully conspiring to make the Red Army fascist in the 30s or turn Pravda into a hotbed of reactionary sentiment. The "system" under which we live — the vast bloated human resources bureaucracy that governs the earth — will not allow such a thing. That is by design. This giant administrative biomass prevents any kind of accountability to the public.

The death of the unitary executive in American political life is a clear example of this phenomenon. Virtually every city in America, for instance, uses some version of the "manager-council" mode of government. The office of mayor, insofar as it exists at all, is generally a functionary with little real power to hire and fire employees or to enforce the law.

For instance, in my own town of Hillsdale, Michigan, the city manager is unelected and makes well over $100,000 a year. He has a contract that keeps him in power for nearly a decade. The city council, on the other hand, while elected, has no meaningful salary and faces constant turnover. The bureaucracy — the manager, clerks, lawyers, etc. — are a faction unto themselves. To give one example, the city council prohibited the recreation department from buying an ice cream machine for the local park snack stand. To do this, they ruled that all transactions over $10,000 had to be voted on by the city council. So, the recreation bureaucrats simply split the purchase of the machine into two transactions and bought it anyway.

All of American life is like this at every level of power. In Michigan, the Governor, Attorney General, and Secretary of State are all elected positions. We have a tripartite executive in which there is no final accountability for the enforcement of the laws. When I was in the Corps, I never once saw the battalion commander come down to the offices of the lower echelons. He was always in meetings, always busy, always somewhere else. When Biden says he did not know of the Mar-a-Lago raid, I believe him. The only decision he is allowed to make each day is about what flavor pudding cup he gets for lunch. Make no mistake, Donald Trump was in a similar boat. When he ordered American troops to leave Syria, the Pentagon went into revolt. One must not also forget the coup after January 6, in which members of Congress and the Joint Chiefs of Staff worked together to prevent Trump from exercising his lawful authority.

Alexander Hamilton describes the Presidency in *The Federalist*: "Energy in the Executive is a leading character in the definition of good government." He goes on to argue that the qualities of energy are unity of powers, duration in office, adequate provision for personal support, and possession of competent powers.

This type of office does not exist today and this is intentionally so.

The Founders' vision of American government was manly and assertive. This is why they speak of energy, unity, strength, and power. The modern deep state, though powerful, is feminine and passive-aggressive. It lacks unity and energy precisely in order to thwart a potential takeover by a man of strength and vision. It is stultifying and bloated on purpose.

Infiltration of this system by manly and assertive young men is almost certain to be unsuccessful. These types will be shunted aside, pressured, and ground to dust wherever possible. I saw this in my own time in the Marine Corps. The Corps shuffles officers and personnel around constantly. Every two or three years one can expect another "Permanent Change of Station," ostensibly intended to encourage a "broad range of career experience" but more importantly, to prevent the formation of tightly knit units loyal to strong leaders.

Though a competent officer, well-liked by many of my peers, and strictly professional with my superiors, I was "not right" for the institution. They could smell it on me. I was, for instance, forced to submit to multiple "talking tos" from higher ranking officers. One complaint — lodged by a morbidly obese enlisted female Marine who felt I had smirked at her — ended with an hour-long meeting with said female Marine in which her commander, a Major, concluded by insisting to me that though he couldn't prove I had done anything wrong (I hadn't), it was important to ensure that she felt "listened to" because this was a "new Marine Corps."

Every institution in American life is spiritually gay.

The only solution is to clear the ground — to "deconstruct" the system, as the post-modernists say, and start over. Christopher Rufo gave a wonderful talk at Hillsdale College this past year entitled "Laying Siege to Our Institutions." This is the right mindset.

We cannot save our corrupt regime from the inside. The Right does not have the personnel, time, or unity of purpose to stage its own decades-long march through the institutions. Instead, we must actively work to undermine their legitimacy and purpose — especially when it comes to those organs that act as the sword and shield of the regime. The FBI is the enemy. The Pentagon is the enemy. The NSA is the enemy.

The liberal ruling class depends on white men with guns to secure itself. It is imperative that we deny it access to this crucial resource. Demoralization propaganda and spiritual warfare in the public square are critical to this effort. We must make it so that the toadies of the regime face constant embarrassment and mockery everywhere they turn. The work of the anons on Twitter and elsewhere is of the utmost importance in this regard.

There is a place, too, for those like me, Christopher Rufo, and others who write openly under their own name. There are dangers, of course. It is much easier to corrupt a man with money and honor when you know his name. But the men of the Right should not reflexively fear to associate themselves with right-wing principles in public. The costs of explicitly identifying oneself as a "true patriot" and "radical moderate centrist," as I consider myself, are not intrinsically prohibitive.

I believe in the need for a return of industry at home, an end to the empire abroad, and dramatic cuts to immigration. I think the government should outlaw genital mutilation of children and crack down on violent crime. These are explicitly right-wing positions, yes, but they are also popular positions. I do not fear associating myself with them.

Infiltration is of the utmost difficulty, but outright assaults on the weak points of the ideological front can work well. Donald Trump's campaign in 2015 is the model. He may not have been able to govern effectively but the blow he struck in the spiritual war was of the utmost importance.

Boldly stating the truth is an aristocratic trait.

I am not suggesting that this openness is a model for everyone on the Right. Nor am I suggesting that young men should not go to college or get a high-paying or influential job if it is available. But we also should not delude ourselves. The pressing task is not to infiltrate the institutions or to grift off them, but to bring them down. A man who depends on a thing for his livelihood creates an incentive for himself *not* to work for its destruction.

It is simply in the nature of many young men to work hard, even when such work is not good. Men who have been bred for generations to hold duty and truthfulness in the highest regard will find it hard *not* to empower the very system that desires to destroy them. Their conscientiousness is a weakness.

The Interahamwe Left and its murderous rhetoric is a global threat that is becoming more openly radical. It is necessary for some to oppose them in the open and for others to work from the shadows—but all must aim for the same target.

Strength, friendship, and discipline are far greater assets in this spiritual fight than credentials, degrees, and corner offices. It is not necessary for the Right to sit in the seat of power in order to undermine it. Iron is more important than gold. In our time, friendship, strength, and manly virtue are more needed than money and access. The real source of power lies not within the regime, but outside it.